URBAN RIFLE

By

Clint Smith

To all the 0311s and 11 Bravos, and my grandchildren Samantha, Alex, Greyson, and Ashlynn. May their world be calm, and if not may they be stone cold riflemen.

Very special thanks, without these people trust me there would be no book. Heidi, my girlfriend and wife who makes my life possible. Roger Wallace, who made this book possible. George Matthews, who made Thunder Ranch possible.

C.A.S

Table of Contents

Foreword   4

Who are you?   5

Safety   11

Theory   13

Principles   14

Rifle Action Types   16

Elements of Rifle Marksmanship   21

Efficient Manipulation of Fundamentals   24

Factors Affecting Firing Positions   27

Firing Positions   35

Conditions of Carry   50

Methods of Carry   52

Methods of Deployment   58

Malfunctions   63

Administrative Loading and Unloading   70

Fighting Loads: Empty and Tactical   74

Transitions   80

Support Equipment   84

Barricades and Rests   98

Cover and Concealment   104

Target Indicators   109

Camouflage   111

Movement   112

Night Firing Techniques   114

Care and Cleaning   127

Range Drills   131

FOREWORD

The purpose of this book is for teaching. For those who wish to teach themselves and those who want to teach others. By design its condensed size, font, and spacing is made to fit in your range bag so you will have it with you as a reference. It began in the front seat of a van while teaching on the road driving from state to state and coast to coast over 30 years ago. Since those initial pages it has become a living, working document that has seen numerous revisions and updates as the years, equipment, gear, rifles, and engagements have changed or morphed. This is the latest version and it will continue to grow forward. I first heard mention of 'the book' years ago. It was referenced in casual conversation but never seen.

At its inception in 1983 the original course of URBAN RIFLE, in Clint's words, "no one wanted it and it couldn't be given away for free." Since then it has become the cornerstone of the school and a course that has been replicated and often copied by others. It has taken on many names or variations, but large sections of the content owe its lineage to that course from 1983. Rarely is there an opening in an Urban Rifle course these days at Thunder Ranch Oregon. In the last 17 years that I have known him in various capacities –teacher, coach, mentor, boss, and friend, Clint has continued his daily commitment to his students. With brutal honesty at all times he says he has no delusions that he will live forever but that the content he teaches becomes ours and our job is to pass it on and pass it on correctly and safely. This book is a part of that commitment. It truly compiles a lifetime of teaching and inspiring others to teach. Two words are often used interchangeably when it comes to firearms. The first is Instructor, the second is Teacher. They mean completely different things. A lot of us are Instructors but we should aspire at all times to be Teachers. Anyone can buy a red shirt, but it is not about you. It is about them.

Roger Wallace, June 2016

Chapter 1

USERS: WHO ARE YOU?

This book addresses the theory and usage of the rifle necessary for developing the skills needed to use the rifle effectively in all environments. This book's scope includes rifle use for law enforcement officers, the military and people from the private sector. Some would have you believe there is a different style or technique of using the rifle for each occupation. There is not. A fight is a fight — behind a squad car, a sand dune or inside a doorway in your home. Let there be no misunderstanding, even in today's world with its need to be "politically correct," the ultimate goal in a fight is to win. <u>PERIOD.</u> This book addresses the use of the rifle to win in all environments, including the more likely short-range engagements.

THE POLICE

With the urbanization of our environment and the attendant problems of more crime, drugs, and well-armed criminals and terrorists, a transition to a more efficient and effective weapon system is needed. As a society, our attraction and attachment to handguns is based on the American past, on the convenience of a handgun, and probably on a basic misunderstanding of the handgun's limits. If we all truly understood the role of a handgun in the chain of fighting tools we would all be more aware of just how poor a choice it is; hence the rifle.

The police carry handguns as defensive tools and symbols of authority, in the same vein as their badge. If we learned from the past, we would know most handgun gunfights take place at short ranges. The fight will probably be, and has historically been, no different if you have a rifle in your hands. Police officers have been, and will be, in fights with rifles inside what they would normally consider pistol range.

A law enforcement officer's job requires many tasks, one of the most important being the positive identification of a potential threat when the occasion arises. Often (usually?) the only way to positively identify a potential threat is to be close enough to see it, or more correctly, to see the threat's hands and weapons. Even law enforcement precision riflemen using scopes, where average shots are only 50 to 75 yards, can have difficulty confirming targets. Hence, the need for officers to often close to "toe-to-toe" ranges before a fight even starts.

Probably one of the most vivid examples of a rifle being used in a confrontation is the 1986 Miami FBI shootout. This now decades old incident had a remarkable effect on American law enforcement. Most have heard the joke about bringing a knife to a gunfight. The Miami incident was not a joke. It was, however, a good example of bringing shotguns and handguns to a rifle fight.

Fortunately, numbers prevailed, but not before a terrible toll was exacted on the FBI agents. The surviving members of that stake-out team recall the devastating psychological and physiological impact the rifle used by their opponent had on them at those deadly short ranges. Add to the Miami incident, the North Hollywood bank robbery (a sustained rifle fight), Waco, and the former police officer Christopher Dorner's murderous rampage in Southern California and you can get a good idea of what law-enforcement officers are facing today. And there will be more of it in their future.

The idiosyncrasies of urbanization, along with general law enforcement's failure to properly train with shotguns, has created a trend to dump shotguns in favor of rifles. The thought seems to be that rifles are easier to shoot, train with and possess less recoil. A shotgun training program of 5 or 25-rounds a year does not need to be replaced by a rifle. A shotgun program of this caliber needs simply to be corrected and turned into a real shotgun program — and if that's not possible, DROPPED ENTIRELY.

However, if a law enforcement agency's replacement rifle program is not going to be any more effective than its currently poor shotgun training, they should save the taxpayers — and themselves — the money and trouble of trying to change. The end results are directly proportional to the amount and quality of effort invested. ***Do not assume a training problem can be "fixed" with a simple influx of technology***. Think about it.

And a last thought for law enforcement: I have been approached with the "Put rifles in the 'sergeants and lieutenants' cars" concept. It is my limited understanding that many (most?) sergeants and lieutenants are part of the "management team," and are often not in the field a great deal of the time. I believe it would be better to have pre-designated, rifle-assigned marksman (issued weapons and trained prior to the problem) to use for containments, perimeters and as active-shooters, etc. Let the sergeants and lieutenants "manage". This concept is in effect in some agencies, like the "PRT" or Primary Response Team concept in which patrol officers have SWAT status and respond to initial calls to contain the scene or engage shooters until the full team can respond.

About 80% of all police departments in the United States have less than twenty-five officers. Common sense dictates the smaller departments may have to address serious threats with all hands on board. That said, having a rifle in hand doesn't equate to competency and whoever has it better train up to a high level of competency.

THE MILITARY
Unlike the police, the general military establishment does not have much use for a handgun. Due to a general lack of handgun training programs in the past, handguns usually serve no other purpose than a symbol of authority or a badge of rank in the military, similar to the police. The military use of the rifle, as based on their training programs, is geared for

longer ranges of 100 to 500 yards, or thereabouts. The longer the range the better they like it, since distance gives them room to appropriately work their supporting fires from the air and ground units. In Afghanistan, our opponents intentionally stand outside of our effective small arms range further creating the impression that long range shooting is the future.

The problem develops when we consider what most confrontation ranges traditionally have been. Consider the range when clearing trenches in France in 1917, caves at Okinawa, bunkers at Omaha beach or defending against mass infantry attacks in Korea in the 1950's. More recently, the Marines engaged in house-to-house fighting in the Imperial City of Hue in 1968, and troops cleared buildings in Kuwait City and Baghdad as well as the alleys of Somalia. Long-range rifle fire is certainly stressful to receive, and its effectiveness at long range can be frightening. But most military rifle applications have usually occurred at short ranges, and continued urbanization dictates that it will be the norm in the future.

The military application equals free fire zones, right? — wrong! Consider that conservatively 20 to 25 percent of all casualties are from friendly fire of one kind or another. In trenches, blockhouses and urban areas, fighting can be at short range against moving targets obscured by smoke, flying debris and against enemy troops who are willing to use protective cover. I strongly advocate the use of protective cover and concealment, with training that emphasizes covering fire drills, movement to cover, and acquiring the best firing positions that will still be functional under the duress of combat. Most importantly, training should include intense marksmanship and manipulation exercises.

Rifle Technology
Potential rifles of the next century "MAY" have capabilities we haven't even dreamed of yet. There are already designs that include the ability to fire conventional .223 caliber ammunition from one barrel with a second

barrel/magazine option that uses a 20 mm air-bursting round — all regulated by a variable fuse adjusted by laser range finder and on-board computer chips. With attachments, the rifle can be stuck around corners to "see" and shoot.

And we thought Starship Troopers were exotic! However, this had better be a great rifle at the stated $15,000 price tag. I can see it now, "Here private, this is your $15,000 rifle." I guess we've come a long way since the $18 price tag of the M-1 Grease guns of World War II.

Hopefully, we are not outsmarting the poor "grunt" who carries, walks, fights and wins most wars with a rifle in his — or her — hands. We can bomb the place into a parking lot, but we don't own it until an infantryman stands on it.

Past, current, and developing concepts of the military include the Army's "Land Warrior" and the Marine Corps "Urban Warrior" programs or whatever the current in vogue warfighter thing is. Whatever we call them, hopefully they are addressing marksmanship and military operations in urban terrain, as well as the R&R (Rifles & Radios with extra batteries) concept for infantry (Land Warrior and Urban Warrior have been rejected by the various services at this time, but parts of the systems are being field tested, so we will see what comes of all this money spent on exotic technology).

The Private Sector
All of the previous information about the police and military should be of interest to the civilian rifle owner. "The wise person learns from the experience of others — only a fool learns from experience." Everything advocated for the police and military goes double for private citizen rifle owners. *You more than anyone had better hit your target, because you will probably not get any backup, and it may be some time before the "supply chopper" arrives.*

Probably the biggest threat to the private sector is just maintaining personal ownership of rifles. If you are going to use a rifle, use it effectively. How well it is used and controlled (responsibly owned) by the private sector, will affect how long they will be AVAILABLE to be owned by individuals.

The private sector ownership of rifles can be put into proper perspective. In the days after the Iraqi withdrawal from Kuwait City, you might have noticed CNN footage showing all of the civilians picking up "dropped" rifles. Even in the interviews, the people said they were "picking them up and storing them so if they ever were invaded again they could shoot back." Citizen groups in the Ukraine are calling for their own version of the 2nd Amendment, as well as citizens of Venezuela and Columbia. There's a moral in there somewhere!

A Short Political Observation
The United Nations and United States have an ongoing policy of trying to enact or invoke private-sector disarmament. That apparently seems like a good idea… to no one else but them. As a planet and a people, we have had other "world peace organizations" that were going to save us from ourselves. A good example is the League of Nations, which didn't do Ethiopia much good in 1936 or Poland in 1939. The current "United Nations" also hasn't done much for the millions of people butchered in Africa or Southeast Asia, going back to the 1950's. Don't ask someone to do for you what you're not willing to do for yourself.

Chapter 2

SAFETY

Contrary to popular belief and myth, safety rules are not just for the range. We use them on the range because they work there to create a safe environment in which to train, and they give us disciple and organization. **<u>The primary purpose for safety rules is to use them in a fight, or combat</u>**, you choose the word that applies. Safety at the range shouldn't be a big deal; gun handling in fight might be critical to everyone involved.

YOU are responsible for your own actions. The best two safeties to use with any weapon are:

1. YOUR HEAD: Use it — and think about what you're doing.
2. KEEPING YOUR FINGER OFF THE TRIGGER.

These two thoughts, used with the following rules, will successfully prevent **ALL** accidental, negligent, unauthorized or uncalled-for discharges:

1. TREAT ALL GUNS AS IF THEY ARE ALWAYS LOADED.

2. NEVER POINT THE MUZZLE AT ANYTHING YOU ARE NOT WILLING TO DESTROY.

3. KEEP YOUR FINGER OFF OF THE TRIGGER UNTIL YOUR SIGHTS ARE ON THE TARGET AND YOU ARE WILLING TO SHOOT.

4. BE SURE OF YOUR TARGET AND THE BACKSTOP BEYOND IT.

To have a negligent discharge people must violate these rules. People can say what they want: "Oh don't worry, it's not loaded." People can do what they want: "We prep the trigger." [Take-up "slack"]. Then when they have a negligent discharge they will blame *everything* that goes wrong on *everybody and everything else*. They will also be guilty of STUPIDITY — which still isn't a felony but often leads to litigation. There is a trend now to dismiss proper gun handling and muzzle control in the name of "because we are professionals and cool we can cover each other with muzzles and don't need to use safety rules", and so on. Actually, "because we are professionals" is exactly the reason we should control our muzzles. Use and practice the four safety rules!

Another way to put this is...how many people do you know that you would trust behind you with a loaded gun in a gunfight?

Apply the four safety rules constantly and with vigor. Be responsible for *your* own actions.

"Stupid is as stupid does." –Forrest Gump

Chapter 3

THEORY

The use of the rifle in short range, 0 to 100 yard, environments is generally overlooked altogether in most training programs. The fact remains that most rifle confrontations take place *under 100 yards*. This should point out a serious flaw in many (or even most) instruction programs. The student or teacher, either by instruction or through personal research, should be aware that rifles are used a great deal *inside* what is generally considered effective handgun ranges. Let's say that again. *The overwhelming majority of rifle fights take place at common handgun ranges.*

The advantages of the rifle are clear. A distinct increase in power and terminal effectiveness on the target, an increased magazine capacity (to reduce manipulation, not to "spray" the target), and a longer sight radius for precise aiming, are just some advantages. Its disadvantages remain similar to other weapons. The rifle's need for manipulation, reloading, leading with the muzzle in tactical applications and retention, can possibly all be disadvantages when compared to handguns.

The biggest challenge is to make yourself aware of these pros and cons and then to capitalize on the pros. You must be able to fire from an effective platform, manipulate, load, clear and keep the weapon in service *quickly*. But above all, you must understand the purpose of shooting is to *hit*! You must get hits to solve the problem and only the *good* hits count.

Chapter 4

PRINCIPLES

The conventional rifle may be categorized by the following points:

- It's individually carried and serviced. One person can transport it and keep it working.
- Of shoulder-mounted configuration, the weapon should be capable of aimed, controlled fire that produces reliable hits.

- By choice it should have one-shot, one-hit terminal effectiveness. If the threat is hit with a well-placed, effective projectile, the confrontation should either be over, or at least *significantly altered.*

Urban rifles apply some of the above concepts plus:

- Lightweight: Can you carry this thing all day and all night?

- Mobility: Compact size and weight may affect selection (small and light for one job, big and bold for another).

- Penetration of the projectile: Based on area and geographic environment, is your cartridge and/or projectile an effective combination? Are you under or over-gunned for the job at hand?

- Ease of manipulation: Can you reach and operate the dials, knobs and widgets that make the weapon work?

- Magazine capacity: A large-capacity magazine is a wonderful thing, **if it's used effectively**. When your rifle is going "bang" down-range, you may be hitting your target, you may be making your target duck, you may or may not be winning, but you are definitely unloading that magazine. Use the rounds available effectively to get hits. The 20 to 30- round magazines are good because **used effectively** they reduce manipulation and allow you to keep your muzzle down-range longer so you can protect yourself with *less* down-time. **The big magazine is not so you can shoot more, but so you can manipulate *less* AND STAY IN THE FIGHT!!!**

Chapter 5

RIFLE ACTION TYPES

There are many variations of rifle actions, both classic and modern. Our concern here is with current basic types. First and foremost, never under estimate the potential effectiveness of *any* action type. Some say "The bolt action is slow to load and operate". Maybe... maybe not. In the hands of a skilled operator, a bolt-action rifle will go a long way toward keeping everyone honest at its business end. Historically, if a target is hit every time the bolt action is fired, the targets will soon have a tendency to lose interest in the person running that rifle. There are other variations other than the examples given, but the point we make should be clear.

To help illustrate the concept, there is just one photo of each general type of rifle, along with a brief opinion of the strengths and weaknesses of each type. There are many other weapons systems and calibers other than those shown, so each person should make a selection based on research, experience and personal requirements. A sound Winchester Model 94 may indeed be a better choice for you than a poorly made semi auto or bolt gun. The variables are almost countless and you need to add them all up prior to making your decision.

BOLT ACTION (Fig. 1)

There's no arguing that quality bolt actions are mechanically strong. They are the most consistently accurate, although for the untrained they may be slow to load and manipulate. They are available in a wide variety of calibers and the list seems to be growing constantly. Examples of the genre are the Remington 700 series, Ruger M-77 and the classic Winchester M-70, to name just a very few. In the custom rifle mode, none are better than G.A. Precision. They are many more makers of varying quality and construction; you simply need to look for what you're after.

SEMI-AUTOMATIC of military origin (Fig. 2)

These designs are usually tested and proven with large sums of taxpayer money, and their mettle is often additionally tested in the battlefield at the cost of lives. The military semi and full-automatic actions usually go through several changes over a period of years to reach final effectiveness. For example, the M-16 began life very different from the current generation A-4 and M-4 series. These weapon "systems" provide for rapid second shots for multiples hits or for multiple target engagements, as might be expected in military confrontations. Examples include the AR-15/M16, AK-47, M1/M14, SKS and a host of others.

SEMI-AUTOMATICS of civilian origin (Fig. 3)

The civilian versions of our battle-proven semi-automatics are usually dressed in polished wood with a nice blued finish. Modern design ideas and finishes have often created designs that show small resemblance to their ancestors, but are, nonetheless, often based on prior military design ideas. For the average hunter, these "civilianized" semi autos are acceptable, but they generally *do not* hold up well under the rigors of heavy field use. Magazine releases and magazines are most often the weak link in the system.

PUMP ACTIONS (Fig. 4)

A few years back there was a trend to push pump action rifles because of their similar mechanical operation with the familiar pump shotguns that dominate domestic hunting fields. Yes, they work alike, and the slide or pump action rifle will probably be functional for the average hunter or weekend shooter. However, the actions, magazines and magazine release are, simply put, inadequate for rigorous use. They have tended to wear out quickly and be unreliable performers. There has been a resurrection of sorts of pumps by Remington with the 7615 pump action model designed for the law-enforcement market.

LEVER ACTION (Fig. 5)

Lever-guns have been around for well over a century, and then some. Indeed, there are several strong points to a lever gun design. They are generally ambidextrous. They use reasonably powerful cartridges and have a larger magazine capacity than most semi auto or pump actions of civilian persuasion. They are strong, compact and usually very handy. Many students at Thunder Ranch have used lever actions of various models during the three-day *Urban Rifle* course with good success. The shooters were able to effectively engage targets, shoot, move, and communicate right along with the AR's and other "fancy" rifles. Additionally, some models, like the Winchester 1886 and Marlin 1895, use highly effective cartridges, like the powerful .45-70, and can be a serious force to be reckoned with. An issue to be aware of with the lever action is carrying the rifle in Condition One, *round in the chamber,* can be a strain, both mechanically and mentally, and requires an understanding of the proper and safe release of the hammer to the rest position.

SINGLE SHOT (Fig. 6)

Sharps, Hi-walls, Ballards and the like are the rifles legends are made of.
From the infamous Billy Dixon shot at Adobe Walls, Texas, where legend
has it buffalo hunter Dixon killed an Indian at 1,500 yards, to the
decimation of the buffalo herds. These rifles with powerful, effective
cartridges are remarkably under-estimated. Don't make that mistake. I've
seen my good friend Mike Venturino make first-shot hits on steel torso
targets at a measured 700 yards with his single shot 45-70. I'd say there's
a lesson there somewhere.

Chapter 6

ELEMENTS OF RIFLE MARKSMANSHIP

When people leaf through a book, they most always skip the chapter on the fundamentals because they are "boring" and want to get to the "fast and fancy" stuff. I suggest you read Chapter One then Chapter Six, then Chapter Two then Chapter six, etc., throughout the entire book. By doing this little drill, you'll more than likely absorb the salient points whether you want to or not — and you will likely retain the things that will help you *survive* in a confrontation. You can fake it for a while, but if you haven't mastered the basics, eventually you will fail at everything else. Seriously!

There are three elements of rifle marksmanship: **AIM, HOLD AND SQUEEZE**.

1. AIM (Aiming): Consisting of two parts:

1a. SIGHT ALIGNMENT
Aiming is the alignment of the sights, front and rear to themselves (Fig. 7). NOTE: The top of the front sight is centered in the available rear aperture.

Fig. 7

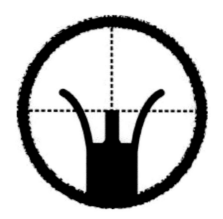

1b. SIGHT PICTURE

This is the alignment of the sights to the target, based on the available center of mass, movement and distance to the target, or how well you can see the target (Fig. 8). Proper alignment of the sights to themselves and when overlaid on the target can produce effective hits if the other elements of equal importance are considered and used — things like trigger squeeze and breathing, for instance.

Fig. 8

Sight Picture

2. HOLD (Holding): Consisting of two parts:

2a. The *hold* of the rifle is maintaining the rifle in the most stable platform with the purpose to reduce movement of the sights, thus enhancing the possibility of an accurate hit on the target. Platform stability is based on the position used, e.g. prone, whether or not the shooter is deployed with a loop sling, bipod or rested on a bench or other stable object. *Hold* comes from the physical contact between you and the weapon, so physical conditioning effects hold. Your breathing, heart rate and mobility needed to get into strongly supported positions all effect your ability to *hold* well.

2b. *Holding* is the act of maintaining the sights on the target (aim) to cause proper projectile/bullet placement.

3. SQUEEZE (Squeezing): Also called: *press, compress, surprise break, stroke* and other terms.

Whichever term is used, the key is to cause the hammer or striker to fall on the primer and the weapon to fire without disrupting the hold and holding elements — thereby causing the projectile to hit the target accurately. It seems obvious, but a reminder **NOT TO YANK ON THE TRIGGER** is always in order. Yanking on the trigger moves the sights (aim) and platform (hold) and causes misses. Perhaps no single event can affect the accuracy of your shot as much as the skillful application of a correct trigger stroke. This is a skill that must be mastered.

Chapter 7

EFFICIENT MANIPULATION OF FUNDAMENTALS

Manipulation is very simple. We want to load, reload, clear a stoppage, or unload with the least amount of movement. In simple terms, the more efficiently you move, the smoother you are. The smoother you are the quicker it's done. Reduction of movement is reduction of time. The adage "**SMOOTH IS FAST**" is correct.

That this whole "manipulation" idea is so important is why it's included early in the book. This way, from the very beginning, you can begin to consider the concepts as you start to deploy the rifle. You can start hard-wiring your body-memory-motion-synapses all over again, only this time, you'll be doing it the right way.

Something to think about is your ability to stay in the fight. If I were loading, reloading, or clearing a stoppage, I would be "unplugged" from the fight — which means I'm a target. You're either shooting back with solid hits, or you're a target. It's as simple as that.

First, as you begin to manipulate the rifle, get as much cover and concealment as possible and keep the muzzle pointed in the direction of the threat. We keep the threat covered as we manipulate because as soon as I'm back "in service" I'll want to shoot if the need arises. Keep your shooting hand in a place where, as soon as the rifle is loaded or fixed, your hand can do the work needed to shoot. The strong hand would be kept in a firing grip, with the trigger finger **OFF THE TRIGGER** if not shooting or if off-target. Your opposite hand would remove old magazines if needed (on the M-16/AR-15 the trigger finger releases the magazine), work the action (on the M-16/AR-15 the curled left index finger releases and pulls the charging handle rearward), seat new magazines, clear stoppages, and other administrative duties as-required.

Heckler & Koch products are designed to work this way, using the left hand. However, on M1/M14, Mini-14s, and AK your left hand and arm cross *under* the magazine to work the charging handle to the rear. Try it, it works great, and keeps your trigger-finger where it belongs, **OFF THE TRIGGER**. All of this is done with the butt of the rifle kept at the shoulder and the eyes and muzzle in the target area. Even if you're empty, they may not know it or the ammunition fairy may bring you a loaded magazine. It could happen...

Remember; if something in your status changes, like your ammo supply or a stoppage, the last thing you want to do is take your eyes off of your hard-won target. To clarify a point, this means you should keep your head and eyes up so you can see the target and/or the target area. *It doesn't mean to put your head up so you can get hit*. If rounds are incoming, get out of the way. Remember what Forest Gump had to say about being stupid.

Also — and a big ALSO here — practice loading drills and stoppages. You probably don't submerge your rifle in water or cover it with mud, dirt, or snow when you go to the range, so it probably always works. Did you see the photos of those soldiers in Iraq with about a pound of sand on their rifles as they moved out in a sand-storm? Gunfights are not usually held at the range. Thus, if rounds are incoming, *Get down — or you will get hit*. If you get down or use cover, and you should, you subject the rifle to the elements, which can cause stoppages. Dirt and debris may clog up the action.

Practice loading, unloading and stoppage clearances from all positions — *every* time you go to the range. It's the cheapest insurance you'll ever get. Remember, I doubt that Allstate Insurance — the "Good Hands People" — will be there to bail you out. Rely on your own hands to do any bailing out required. Also, remember to use cover. People shoot you because they see you. They see you because you let them. Don't let them see you!

Practice until you can clear stoppages smoothly. Don't rush. Fast comes with smooth. I have never ever met anyone who saw a stopwatch present in a gunfight...ever.

Chapter 8

FACTORS AFFECTING FIRING POSITIONS

The basics of rifle marksmanship would be incomplete without including the elements that detail the firing position. There are seven points, each of equal importance, each contributing to the effectiveness of the firing position and bullet placement.

1. OPPOSITE HAND (Left hand for right-handed shooters)
The left hand may be far enough forward to assist in absorbing recoil by contacting the forward sling swivel. The fingers are *not* closed tight, but are relaxed in a natural curl. Most importantly, the placement of the hand, forearm, and elbow are critical. The bones of the hand, forearm, elbow, knee, leg and foot are *under* the rifle to provide skeletal support.

2. BUTT TO SHOULDER (In the pocket)

Placement of the rifle butt into the pocket, which is formed between the rotary-joint of the shoulder and the collar bone, is critical. Butt placement should be consistent for each shot. Sounds simple, but this is a commonly violated principle. Set the butt the *same* for each shot to help assure repeatable performance, both from the rifle -and from you.

3. STRONG-HAND PLACEMENT (And pressure) (Fig 8.3)

Your strong-hand placement should be as high as possible on the stock gripping surface. The placement and pressure of "hold" should be consistent from shot to shot. On conventional stocks, the lower three fingers should grasp and *pull* firmly to the rear, with the thumb straight along the action. Pistol-grip stocks should have the hand as high as practical with the hand held as if holding a ball bat.

Fig 8.3

Fig 8.4

4. STRONG ELBOW (Right-handed shooter's right elbow) (Fig 8.4)
Strong elbow placement is important since it effects placement of the butt to the formed shoulder pocket. Whenever support is available (like the ground in prone, a tree, or a ledge) use it and get that elbow firmly grounded on it. If there is no support — if you have to shoot offhand — try to keep the arm parallel to the ground (stick out the elbow to the side) to help keep a pocket for the butt.

5. BREATHING
Breathing is another body function hard to control in a fight. It's probably best for the novice (or everybody) to at least work on the *respiratory pause*. That's the moment or two *between* breaths where body movement due to breathing *isn't* moving the rifle sights. This breathing pause can be a useful and critical bit of time occurring and an opportunity if you learn how to control it.

6. RELAXED BODY
Okay, so it's pretty hard to be relaxed in a gunfight. The actual meaning here is to have those body parts not actively involved in being part of the firing platform add as little movement as possible to the equation. The moral here is don't flop your feet around while firing. If you're not actively using some part of your body, it needs to be relaxed and still.

7. STOCK WELD
The stock weld is where your face meets the rifle stock. This placement should be as consistent as possible. Stock weld affects eye relief, which affects what we see through the sight, be they glass or iron. For consistent groups, placement *must* be the same each time. Stock weld location may vary in different positions, but should be consistent for *that* position. (Fig 8.5)

Fig 8.5

SUPPLEMENTS TO MARKSMANSHIP

BREATHING

There is much discussion over which breathing technique is best. There are three things you can do — and one thing you shouldn't do. Three common breathing techniques are:

* Inhale and hold
* Exhale and hold
* Exhale half a breath and hold

These breathing techniques allow you to aim, hold steady, and squeeze the trigger without your moving chest mucking-up the sight picture. Pick the one you like, and I recommend you try all three methods before you decide. **The one thing you shouldn't do is to breathe and shoot at the same time**. As you inhale or exhale your sights do the "Macarena" and that isn't exactly conducive to hitting the target with any degree of regularity. Needless to say, any movement is a bad idea. I've actually seen people try to chew gum and shoot rifles at the same time. Go figure.

Fig 8.6

NATURAL POINT OF AIM

A "natural point of aim" is one using a firing position that considers aim, hold, squeeze and the seven position factors affecting the fired shot, in such a manner that the body — through skeletal support — all work together to keep the sights on-target. After acquiring the target, sight movement (while breathing) should have the sights moving gently in a "12 o'clock to 6 o'clock" pattern. Sort of an "up and down" pulse, that matches your breathing. If you close your eyes and continue to breathe, and then open your eyes, your sights should not have moved off-target to the right or left. If they do move, adjust your whole position (go over those seven factors, etc.) until you can do the "eyes off" drill without pulling the sights off-target. *Now* you have the body's natural point of aim based on skeletal support, not muscle support. After all, a solid base using bones is much more reliable than a "wiggly" one using muscles and tendons. In other words, would you rather use a block of strawberry Jell-O™, or a nice rock, for a rifle rest?   (Fig 8.6)

FOLLOW THROUGH

Once the sights have been placed on-target and trigger compression is started, you need to press-through until the rifle fires. As it fires, you focus on the sights, and follow the sights though recoil, reacquiring them as they come back on-target. There may be other techniques used by marksman for target acquisition purposes, but not all of them are, I believe, appropriate for fighting. The follow-through I describe is, in my opinion, the correct one. Always anticipate that what we are going to shoot is *not* going to go down, be stopped, destroyed, or whatever. Be ready to hit the target again if it's needed. Just because you shoot it, doesn't mean your target is going to hear your logical internal discussion as to the outcome of the shot. The target may, indeed, beg to differ with your opinion of what needs to occur next!

STRONG POINT OF INTEREST

How you "run" the trigger is a very critical point and it requires a great deal of attention to detail. A rearward finger compression without dragging the trigger left or right in the housing makes a lot of difference down range. Remember to manipulate the trigger straight to the rear when firing. Many people have been killed by someone they have already killed who isn't dead yet.

Chapter 9

FIRING POSITIONS

Applying firing positions falls into two categories: first, range applications unaltered by terrain or the duress of confrontation; second, actual use applications affected by terrain, rests, supports, cover or concealment, and the right of way for incoming fire. These positions, affected by environment, provide the platform for the shot fired at our opponent. Always keep in mind that poor position selection can provide our threat with opportunities to hit us. We know that the shot fired is only as good as the platform it comes from, so the dilemma is how to get the best platform with the least amount of exposure. **Maximum them, minimum me**!

After teaching for many years, I find that in reality "field positions" fall into three types of uses. **Primary positions** are ones most likely to be used. **Secondary positions** you should be aware of and capable of firing from because you can gain access to a lot of additional targets. **Special positions** are limited in use, but are needed in critical problem areas like assaults, for downed officer recovery, and weapons retention responses. All of these positions are valid and valuable.

PRIMARY POSITIONS (pristine format)
Positions you are most likely to use.

Fig. 9.1

Off Hand (Figs 9.1, 9.2)

The body should be forty-five degrees to the target with the opposite foot forward and feet at least shoulder width apart. The opposite knee is slightly flexed with the body weight leaning slightly forward. The opposite elbow and forearm should be located directly under the rifle. The strong hand should be in a firing grip with the strong elbow up to support rifle butt placement in the pocket of the shoulder. In practice, start with your feet closely spaced together (fig. 9.1), and then step forward into the target as the rifle is mounted (fig 9.2). Keep your head erect and your eyes on the target or target area.

Fig. 9.2

Prone (Figs 9.3)

Starting with the body bladed as in off hand, drop down on both knees. Using your opposite hand (left hand in right handed shooters) to break the fall, let your body go down into full extension. Keep the opposite elbow under the rifle for support. The strong elbow will contact the ground. Feet are at least shoulder width apart with the ankles down to reduce movement and support the platform.

Fig. 9.3

Kneeling Variations

Braced Kneeling (Fig. 9.5) is premeditated kneeling. Braced kneeling requires some set up time. From the bladed position, strong foot back, the opposite foot steps forward and across in front of the strong foot. The foot placement distance is more than shoulder width to provide the width for the base of the tripod like placement of the strong knee and feet. The left foot is one contact point, the right knee and foot being the other two. The right leg is at approximately ninety degrees from the plane of the left leg, and the right foot is under the right buttock with the toes curled under if possible. The back of the left elbow contacts the left knee. A straight downward line is formed with the heel of the hand, the left forearm, left elbow, left knee, shin and foot under and supporting the rifle. The right elbow is parallel to the ground to keep a proper butt pocket for placement of the rifle.

Fig 9.5

Speed Kneeling (Fig. 9.6) is acquired by starting from the bladed position and stepping with the opposite foot (left foot for right hand shooters) forward as in braced kneeling. The primary difference is that the body is lowered to the right knee without lowering the right buttock to contact the right foot. It is, in fact, an upper body off-hand firing position simply lowered to gain use of cover/concealment or to change the angle of attack on a short range threat. The advantage is gained by lowering the profile. Placement of projectiles in the upper half of the available target makes the angle of attack and potential projectile debris exit in an upward plane away from bystanders or unknown backstops.

Fig 9.6

Fig.9.8

Double Kneeling (Fig 9.8, 9.9) can be acquired from the bladed stance. The shooter simply drops down on both knees and sits on both heels. This position allows a great deal of latitude for muzzle depressed environments like in firing down from a roof or muzzle elevated environments for firing up at high angle targets. This latitude extends to firing around cover or concealment like around a building or front of a vehicle.

Fig 9.9

SECONDARY POSITIONS

Olympic Offhand (Fig 9.10A, 9.10B) is valuable because it allows the operator to gain sight plane elevation not available in conventional offhand. This can be a critical issue when using rifles with a parallax offset as with a scope or a mechanical offset on the sight plane of an AR-15/AK47 type sight. Start with the back of your heels shoulder width apart on a line pointing towards the target. Your shoulders should match the line of your feet. The rifle is supported by the fingers of the opposite

42

hand with the elbow directly under the rifle. The strong hand is in its proper place as high and as forward as it can be on the stock with the elbow parallel to the ground. This position is good for a limited number of shots before it needs to be rebuilt because of strain. In competition, this strain is avoided by equipment (jackets, slings special shoes etc.) that provides support for the operator.

Fig. 9.10A

Fig. 9.10B

Sitting (Figs 9.11, 9.12, 9.13) is one of the more stable rifle positions. It is best used on a flat or downhill angle so that the feet are lower than the buttocks. The elbows should contact the knees to support the rifle. Based on individual body size or equipment being carried, the feet and legs can be set up in one of three forms, legs apart (Fig 9.11), legs crossed(Fig 9.12) or legs extended ankles crossed (Fig 9.13).

Fig 9.11

Fig 9.12 Above

Fig 9.13 Below

Squat position (Figs. 9.15, 9.16) is assumed by having the feet spread outside shoulder width apart with the body bladed forty- five degrees from the line of march. The shooter simply allows the body to lower with the buttocks to drop between the legs and the arms to rest inside the legs. The feet should remain flat on the ground.

Fig. 9.15

SPECIALS

Retention positions for use with the rifle can vary to a large degree depending on who is trying to retain the rifle. It is not so much the rifle being retained as the training and physical conditioning of the operator.

Fig 9.16

A military or SWAT operator may defend the rifle with different techniques than the fifty-year old homeowner. Here are some general guidelines. If anyone is attempting to take the rifle by placing their hands (Fig 9.17) on the operator or rifle there should be a **no holds barred** fight. As an operator, I would shoot the threat at any available opportunity. Make every attempt to keep the butt of the rifle on the shoulder and the muzzle between the threat and yourself. Try to keep your feet wide apart and maintain contact with the ground. It's understood that the "shoot the threat" statement may be in conflict with a department policy etc. I don't care. Having been to a couple of police officer funerals, I do not relish the thought of another. If someone is trying to take the rifle from you, regardless of your occupation, shoot him or her. Enough said?

Fig. 9.17

Assault fire, by my definition, is not like most people's perception of the Hollywood *hosing the countryside* technique. Example: a wounded officer is down in the front yard of a rifle-wielding suspect as part of a domestic disturbance call gone bad. SWAT is twenty minutes out, there are three of you there and the wounded officer is apparently in very bad shape. The plan: the first of the three officers is the primary shooter, number two is the secondary shooter, and number three is the recovery officer. Keeping the rifles on the shoulder and selectors on semi-auto the three officers move forward. Any threat or hostile act is met with aimed directed fire at the suspect or immediate area. If the primary shooter has a malfunction or runs out of ammo officer number two, the secondary shooter, takes over. Once past the downed officer, the recovery officer starts back to safety with the wounded officer while officer number one and or two cover themselves as the recovery officer withdraws. Cover or concealment should be used if possible. For those of you who might disagree, consider yourself the wounded officer in the front yard! How did we do?

Chapter 10

CONDITIONS OF CARRY

Conditions of carry reflect the status of the rifle as is carried for use or at rest. The three conditions reflect different stages of preparation or availability for rifle use. Titles reflect recognition of the status of the rifle

Condition One

ACTION Mode. The rifle has a chambered round, the magazine is loaded and in place, safety on. In this mode the rifle is ready for immediate or imminent use. The position of the safety is on but could be off based on the threat's action.

Condition Two

TRANSPORT mode. The rifle has an empty chamber; the magazine is in place and loaded with the safety on. In this mode the rifle may be transported in a rack or lock. It could also be hand carried in this mode while staging or being transported, i.e., in a helicopter. It is imperative that part of all training includes going from this mode to condition one, or making the rifle ready for use. Loading should always be done with the muzzle pointed in a safe direction.

Condition Three

SAFE mode. The rifle has an empty chamber the magazine is removed, action open, safety on. If a rifle is being stored in a vault or case you may be better served to leave the action closed after clearing. For storage in gun vaults remove the magazine then clear the chamber. Keeping the muzzle pointed in a safe direction allow the hammer to go forward in order to release spring tension.

Conditions of carry names vary from organization to organization. It is critical that the muzzle be kept pointed in a safe direction while handling. Although, a remarkably poor idea the daily issuance of long guns to individuals, like issuing rifles to officers at shift changes, is done by some departments. Just some of the issues created by this type of policy can be; is the gun zeroed? Has someone twiddle fiddled with the sights? Who controls the magazines and ammunition? And last but not least, "Well Officer Jones when you shot my client—who was a bystander (or hostage) were you aware of your rifle's zero as well as the mechanical offset of the sights on this model of rifle". And this has HAPPENED a lot and it is going to happen again! All of this is probably worse than the security issue of having individual issued weapons in vehicles.

Chapter 11

METHODS OF CARRY

Working under the premise that you will always carry a rifle more than you will shoot it, the techniques for carry are an important issue. The sling on a rifle is what a holster is to a handgun. Lacking a sling, I'll set it down someplace where I can get to it if I need it!

There are several types of slings available. The current trends are for a carry strap usually made of nylon or the good but old style leather military loop sling. Heckler & Koch and Blue Force Gear offer solid cross body slings based on shooter requirements and mounting options. There are some nylon copies, which people sometimes name after themselves. Sorry guys, but all the copies of the cross body style slings are not a new idea; check out the cross body sling carried by the U.S. Cavalry over a hundred years ago to transport their Spencer's and Trapdoor Springfield's.

Cross body slings are usually best deployed with the head and opposite shoulder though the sling opening. Move the rifle across the body toward the opposite side, away from the strong side secondary weapon so it can be accessed when needed. Tuck it under the opposite armpit while affecting an arrest, etc.

An issue can come up by letting the rifle hang and swing freely. Over the years, I have seen four "accidental" (negligent?) rifle discharges in training. While hanging free, the safety is "swiped" and during movement the trigger is engaged by vest gear. This is not just a training issue; there are documented cases of this occurring in "street" use. When you are done firing, engage the safety, rotate the rifle clockwise and trap it on the chest (Fig. 11.2). Magazine and pistol grip will hold it and insure the safety isn't knocked off by accident. Ambi safeties or left-handed people need to be aware that it is slightly different, but the concept is the same.

Fig. 11.2

DEPLOYING THE RIFLE WITH CONVENTIONAL SLINGS

Strong side carry has the rifle muzzle up over the strong shoulder with the butt of the rifle down (Fig. 11.3). The strong hand grasps the sling about in the center, with the strong forearm parallel to the ground. The dismount requires the opposite hand to move between the sling and the trunk of the body and to grasp the rifle. The rifle is lifted up slightly and moved forward with the muzzle moving towards the threat area (Fig. 11.4, 11.5). The remount requires the opposite hand to grasp the sling near the front swivel as the butt comes off the shoulder. The strong arm is placed between the sling and the rifle as the sling is placed back on the strong shoulder.

Fig. 11.3, 11.4, 11.5

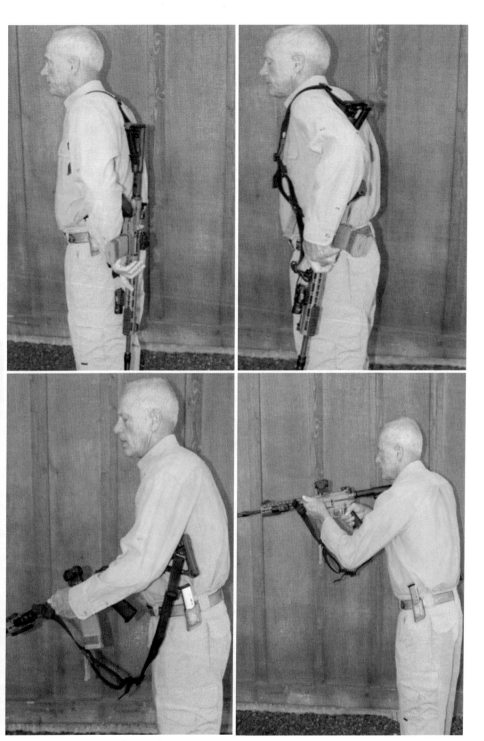

Fig. 11.6, 11.7, 11.8, 11.9

Opposite side carry has the rifle over the opposite shoulder with the muzzle down and butt up (Fig. 11.6). The opposite hand (left hand for right hand shooters) grasps the rifle on or near its forearm. The dismount requires the opposite hand to lift the rifle as the sling comes off the shoulder and the muzzle moves towards the threat area (Fig. 11.6). As the rifle is moved forward, the rifle is rotated counterclockwise between the opposite arm and the trunk of the body while the butt is brought to the strong shoulder (Fig. 11.7, 11.8). The remount requires the opposite hand to grasp the sling at the rear sling swivel. The rifle is rotated outside the arm as the sling slips over the shoulder muzzle down, butt up. (Fig 11.9)

Fig 11.10 Scramble Carry, not good but hands are free.

The scramble carry, although not new, (I've seen this method of carry in old Victory at Sea footage of Marines fighting in the Pacific in WWII) comes from the Scrambler rifle course I designed while Operations Officer at Gunsite in circa 1981. I needed a way to clear my hands to get in the tree at the last firing station. By looping the sling muzzle up over the head it leaves hands and feet free for movement or climbing (Fig.11.9). **IT IS NOT GOOD** for use in close proximity to threats such as searching suspects, etc.

Chapter 12

METHODS OF DEPLOYMENT

Over the years, there have been many attempts to describe different methods of carrying the rifle. Historically, individuals or organizations have projected *Low Ready*, *Guard positions*, *High ready*, and all the variations that people claim to have invented and decided to name after themselves. What is required is the understanding of the concept of how, where and why the rifle being is deployed. Is there imminent danger? Where is the threat or potential threat area? If there is no danger, then sling the rifle. If the conversation then turns to "Well there may be a threat" or "I am in fear of my life!" then unsling the rifle, get the rifle butt on your shoulder, and keep the muzzle between you and the threat (Fig. 12.1). "Won't I get tired?" or "I am tired of carrying the rifle this way." or "How long can I carry it this way?" I would respond to these comments as follows. Only your life may depend on how and where you carry the rifle. Is the muzzle in a place where it can support you in a fight? If you are not in a fight or danger, sling the rifle. If there is a chance there is going to be a fight, or you fear for your safety, then unsling the rifle, put the butt on your shoulder, and keep the muzzle between you and whatever it is you don't like or threatens your safety.

Fig. 12.1

In deployment with the rifle, and in reality all firearms, the position of the muzzle *is not based on technique, it is based on environment.* Keep the butt of the rifle on your shoulder and the muzzle between you and the threat or threat area (Fig. 12.2). If climbing stairs, the muzzle should be pointing at the top of the stairs (Fig. 12.3). If going into a basement, point the muzzle down as you move downward (Fig. 12.4). As you come to a corner, of course you would not want to lead with the muzzle. It may be required to lower the muzzle so as not to project it into the room ahead of you (Fig.12.5). This will allow you to see around the corner as you visually clear slices of the "pie" (the room) with the muzzle in support.

Fig 12.2

Fig.12.3

Fig. 12.4   Fig. 12.5

As you move, search, or work, the ready position keeps the butt of the rifle on your shoulder and the muzzle direction between you and whatever it is you don't like.

Another option for extended movement in areas where there is apparently not an imminent threat may be to use a cross body carry. It "feels" better with pistol grip rifle (AR, AK, FN, HK) but will work with straight stock rifle with practice. The opposite hand holds the forearm area of the rifle while the strong hand grasps the pistol grip area. The butt stock is outside the arm resting on the forearm as the rifle is carried horizontally (Fig. 12.6).   This method is best in a follow the leader, Indian file, or stacked environment. Caution is required so that the muzzle does not cover friendly personnel.

Fig. 12.6

Chapter 13

MALFUNCTIONS

After forty years, it is my personal opinion that the vast majority of weapon malfunctions can be traced back to the operator. Examples include supplying bad ammo, failure to clean, using bad magazines, and using a weapon built from parts or junk rifles. I am amazed at all of the rifles that I have seen that don't work. It's even more amazing that anyone would own a rifle that doesn't work well and all of the time! I would always take a bolt-action rifle that always worked over a semi-automatic that worked sometimes.

One type of malfunction that can occur is from a failure to feed from the magazine. The response then is a "bang" as the rifle fires the first round and is followed by a "click" as the hammer falls on the empty chamber. This failure to fire can occur after the operator does not seat the magazine properly after a loading, or if the magazine release button is hit accidentally. The operator seating or "tapping" the magazine (Fig. 13.1) to seat and lock the magazine and then pulling down on the magazine (13.2) before removing the hand to insure a proper lock up cures this "malfunction." The operator then "racks" or reciprocates the charging handle to load (Fig. 13.3). If there is still a threat the operator should then engage the threat with fire.

Fig. 13.1

Fig. 13.2

Fig. 13.3

If the operator has a failure to fire and runs the "tap- rack" response and still has a failure to fire (Fig. 13.4) the operator should then remove the magazine (Fig. 13.5) and reciprocate the action several times (Fig. 13.6) or what amounts to unloading and clearing the stoppage. Then reload using "tap-pull down-rack" drill to reload the magazine into the rifle.

Fig. 13.4

Fig. 13.5

66

Fig. 13.6

With different rifle types, different kinds of malfunctions may occur. With the Colt family, sometimes operators will encounter a double feed in the shape of a "V" (Fig. 13.6) as the rifle fails to extract and attempts to reload. This malfunction may require pulling the magazine out and holding the charging handle to the rear with the strong hand while the opposite fingers are placed up into the magazine well (Fig. 13.6) to break the stoppage loose. You may consider moderately striking the butt of the rifle on the ground to loosen the rounds. If you have a retractable stock, you should be guarded to not damage or break the stock while striking it on the ground. In this case, it is best to first compress the stock, complete the strike and clearing, and then extend the stock as you load to get the rifle back into action.

All of these actions should, if possible, occur while using cover and keeping the rifle as horizontal to the ground as possible. This allows the extractor/ejector to work as well as it can. Also, in this plane the largest opening on the rifle, the magazine well, is in a position so that gravity may help debris fall clear from the rifle. Keeping the rifle butt at the shoulder as the malfunction is cleared allows for the rifle to be brought back into action as soon as it is cleared. This may be modified as in the "V" stoppage mentioned before, but the operator should work the rifle butt back to the shoulder as the stoppage is being cleared.

I have a very simple way of teaching/explaining this to people. Think of two things in your mind's eye that go together so when you think of one you think of the other: salt and pepper, bacon and eggs, hamburgers and fries…. By now you should get the point. If your rifle isn't working, then simply run the first part, shall we say the "salt", that is tap, pull down, rack to load, and engage as required. If the rifle still doesn't function (remember to take the safety off) with the "salt" part, then simply go right on into the "pepper" cycle. Unload the rifle and reload the rifle. These two actions must flow together in your head for smooth manipulation. They require practice. They also work.

As the reader can tell, I strongly advocate keeping the rifle to the shoulder as much as possible. This serves two purposes, first having the rifle out of firing position as little as possible, and second keeping the muzzle between the operator and the threat. **The operator's eyes should remain on the threat or in the threat area.** You may spend your whole life waiting for this fight, **but once in the fight why would you willingly take your eyes off the threat?**

I am not and do not advocate *you put your head up in the fight.* I do advocate *you keep your head up* to watch the threat and what is, or may change, in the fight. Incoming fire has the right of way. If fire is coming in, you know the answer! If you lower your head to load or clear malfunction, you may lose visual contact with the threat and it may be a lot harder to find it next time!

As a point of interest you may consider that the better your rifle works, the more you should practice malfunction clearance drills. The last time you went to the range the idiot you saw with the rifle that would only fire one round and jam, knows how to clear stoppages. That's all he does when he goes to the range! You, however spent good money for a rifle and ammo that works...correct?

When you zero and practice with your rifle at the range, the environment is usually weapon and operator friendly, i.e., dry and clear etc. Your fight environment may not be the same; this perfect piece of equipment of yours may be affected by all your "extra" tactical gear, body armor, water, mud, dirt, sand, and blood... which could even be your own! Fights are usually not what we think they will be. They are, in fact, just what they are. Even with the best plans and training, gun fights usually don't come out the way we thought they would! The "thing" about great plans is usually the guy who "thinks of it" doesn't collect the interest on the loan, while, in fact, some other poor son of a bitch on the scene does. Let's see, the Marines at Tarawa, the 1st Battalion, 7th Cavalry in the Ia Drang Valley, the SEALS at Paitilla airfield in Panama, Desert One. Pick one.

Many **good** people have "collected" the interest on the loan of poor planning on the part of some *"not here son-of-a bitch"*. Don't you. Plan for yourself if possible, and plan for something to go wrong.... If it does what will you do next? **Plan to win and train to win!**

Chapter 14

ADMINISTRATIVE LOADING AND UNLOADING

As you acquire additional skills with the rifle through training and practice, you will be required to load and unload the rifle. There are several key points to consider.

- Try to load and unload in a manner consistent with the way you will manipulate the rifle when you are fighting with it. Program good habits in and you will get consistent handling out.
- Keep your finger off the trigger while you load and unload.
- Keep the muzzle pointed in a safe direction while you load and unload.
- Remember that the rifle has the potential to discharge each time you load and unload.
- If you use a Colt AR type rifle, when cycling a cartridge in and out of the chamber always be sure to pick it up and look at the primer. It will have a small dent in it from where the firing pin struck the primer. Keep in mind what has the potential for happening each and every time the primer is "touched" by the firing pin!
- Don't point the muzzle at or near your feet while loading or unloading.
- Don't over load magazines with cartridges. Twenty round magazines should be loaded with no more than eighteen rounds. Thirty round magazines should be loaded with twenty-eight rounds. A fully loaded magazine can be difficult, if not impossible, to seat with the rifle bolt in the forward position.

LOADING

As you hold the magazine in your opposite hand (left hand for right handed shooters), look at or feel the cartridges in the magazine.

Fig. 14.1

The cartridges will be stacked in a staggered manner, right to left, or left to right. Note which side of the magazine the cartridge is on. Holding the rifle in your strong hand, butt to the shoulder, place the magazines into the magazine well, pushing it up to seat it and then pulling down to make sure it has seated and locked. Keep the muzzle in a safe direction and use your opposite hand to pull the charging handle to the rear. When the handle is fully retracted, release it so it moves forward without dragging or impeding forward movement from your hands or fingers. After loading, remove the magazine and look at or feel the cartridges in the magazine. The top cartridge should be opposite of the way it was when the magazine was first seated (Fig. 14.3). This check confirms the original top cartridge is, in fact, chambered in the rifle. Replace the magazine by the push up system to seat and the pull down system to confirm it is locked in place.

Fig. 14.2

Fig 14.3

UNLOADING

Start with the safety on, keeping the muzzle pointed in a safe direction and your finger off the trigger. Next, using your opposite hand, remove the magazine from the rifle. Once the magazine is secured, use your opposite hand to pull the charging handle to the rear, removing the chambered cartridge. Run the bolt to the rear several times to assure the chamber is in the clear. If possible, visually inspect the chamber to make sure it is empty. If you elect to take the safety off and drop the hammer, then KEEP THE MUZZLE POINTED IN A SAFE DIRECTION, anticipating the rifle may discharge! "Empty" firearms have shot many people!

Chapter 15

FIGHTING LOADS: EMPTY AND TACTICAL

There are two realistic and practical methods of loading the rifle while in conflict. These two methods address different areas of a confrontation. Historically, ammunition has played a significant role in the outcome of conflicts. The British failures to distribute ammunition at Isandlwana, and Custer's message to "bring packs," are just two of many failures to have ammunition when needed. This failure to have ammunition available while under fire may not have changed the final outcome of these two events, but it sure couldn't have hurt to have more ammunition available.

Fig. 15.1

EMPTY LOADING

Shooting the rifle until it is empty is not good or bad; it is just a reality of fighting. In a fight you will shoot until you win or until the rifle is empty. *If the rifle goes empty it doesn't mean you are going to die. You are simply in a real good fight. **RELOAD THE RIFLE AND GO ON!!!*** On the Colt AR model, if the rifle goes empty, keep the butt on your shoulder and use the opposite hand to get a new magazine while the strong hand index finger hits the magazine release button (Fig. 15.1).

Fig. 15.2

When the empty magazine drops out (Fig. 15.2), push up and seat the loaded magazine (Fig. 15.3). Then pull down on the magazine to make sure it is locked in place. Using the thumb of the opposite hand, press firmly on the bolt release (Fig. 15.4) allowing chambering of a cartridge from the new magazine. Try to keep your eyes and muzzle on the target area during this process. Incoming fire, which always has the right of way, may dictate your ability to monitor the target and target area.

75

Fig. 15.3

Fig 15.4

TACTICAL LOADING

Tactical loading is used to bring the rifle up to maximum capacity by replacing a partially depleted magazine. In lulls in the conflict, or while being covered by a partner, we want to bring the available ammunition to its highest level, and at the same time conserve or save the partially depleted magazine for possible future use. Keeping the rifle butt to the shoulder and muzzle in the area of the threat, grasp a new magazine in the opposite hand with cartridges up, and projectiles forward. Holding the new fully loaded magazine between the thumb and fingers move it alongside the magazine well on the opposite hand side of the rifle (Fig. 15.5).

Fig. 15.5

Using the strong hand index finger press the magazine release button as your opposite hand, which currently holds the new magazine, also grasps the old magazine and removes it from the rifle in a downward motion. Once the old magazine is removed, move the magazines to the right to align the new magazine underneath the magazine well (Fig. 15.6). Push the new magazine up until it locks; then pull down making sure it is seated and locked. Move the opposite hand and the old partially depleted magazine it is still holding rearward, and place it into a pocket or large pouch. (Fig. 15.7).

Fig. 15.6

Fig. 15.7

It is best to not try and secure the magazine in some tight fitting pouch or carrier. If it doesn't go in easily you will be inclined to drop your head and take your eyes out of the fight. Just shove the magazine in your pocket. Fights are usually won by the last round fired so that partial magazine of ammunition may come in handy later on.

I have one thing to add on the subject of tactical loading. Do not take a rifle apart in the sense of removing a magazine to reload it if, so far in the fight, it has saved your life. I think five rounds in a working rifle are better than twenty-five rounds in a magazine in your pocket or back down the hallway on the nightstand. In the training application, (conservatively) 60% of the people who try a tactical load "screw" it up. If you thought the fight wasn't over why take the rifle apart? If it is working so far why take it apart? An empty rifle is easier to load than a cat juggling contest of magazines both full and partially full. So in other words, don't fix something that is not broke… as in most things in life there are exceptions… but very few in this environment.

Chapter 16

TRANSITIONS FROM PRIMARY TO SECONDARY WEAPONS

Transitions are a shifting of weapons systems to bring a working weapon to bear on an immediate and generally short-range threat.

Depending on your occupation or situation you may or may not have a secondary weapon with you in a confrontation. Secondary weapons are usually handguns carried in a variety of places. The optimum place for a handgun on a rifle operator is securely holstered on the strong side. The two major sling options of conventional slings or cross body slings dictate different types of transitions. These are detailed below. Some other points of interest in transitions are:

- If you have no secondary weapon take advantage of available cover, clear the malfunction, reload, fix bayonets, run, or prepare to fight with available stout objects.

- The choice to transition to your secondary weapon, reload the empty rifle, or clear a jammed rifle is a personal decision based on available equipment and *range* to the threat. How soon will the threat get you?

- Transition training should be conducted at realistic ranges appropriate to where a transition would be effective: muzzle contact to twenty or thirty yards.

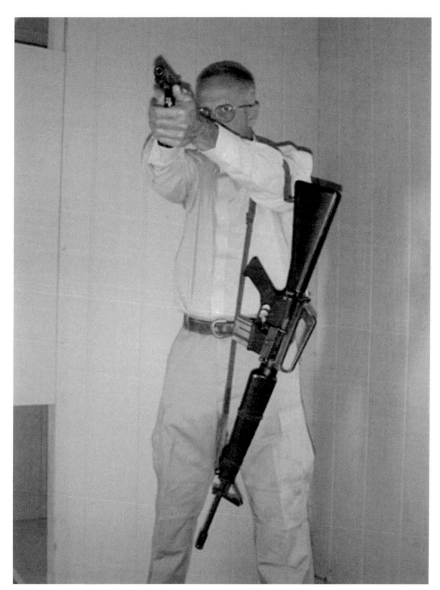

Fig. 16.1

CONVENTIONAL CARRY STRAP

When the primary weapon fails, simply put your opposite hand arm through the opening between the rifle and sling and let the rifle hang muzzle down with the sling resting in the crook of your opposite arm. The strong hand draws the secondary weapon and both hands come together

(Fig. 16.1). After securing the threat you should *reload* your secondary weapon before securing it, then reload or fix your primary weapon.

CROSS BODY SLING

I would recommend that the head and opposite arm be stuck through the open sling. As an example, right handed operators would stick their head, left arm and shoulder through the sling (Fig. 16.2).

Fig. 16.2

When the primary weapon fails, your strong hand should move the rifle under the opposite armpit, which traps the rifle. The strong hand releases the rifle after it is trapped and then moves to the secondary weapon for drawing. After securing the threat, the operator should bring the secondary weapon up to capacity before holstering the weapon and bringing the primary weapon back into service.

Fig. 16.3
NO SLING AVAILABLE
With no sling available, the operator can simply bring the rifle rearward and close to the body as the drawing stroke is implemented (Fig 16.3). A shifting of the lead foot may be helpful to put body weight behind the secondary weapon or to establish a good firing platform (Fig. 16.3).

Chapter 17

SUPPORT EQUIPMENT

There could be a whole book written on support equipment for rifle use. As you read this book someone, somewhere, is making another gadget, good or bad, to hang on a rifle. Remembering that most of your equipment is rarely carried by you (from the truck to the bench, from the truck to the house) the weight and size of the rifle should always be in the back of your mind. Since there is no way I can cover every "widget" made for a rifle, I have elected to break the support equipment down into major categories and have given what is *my* opinion and general experience on these subjects.

SLINGS

There are three common types of slings, carry straps, military loop slings and cross body style slings (Fig. 17.1)

Fig. 17.1

Carry straps are usually made of leather or nylon and are probably the easiest to use in mounting or dismounting on conventional type rifles having standard sling mountings. They generally offer little support if used in firing positions. Slung correctly, carry straps can offer some support in what is termed a hasty sling position (Fig. 17.3) where the opposite arm is stuck through and wrapped around the sling and then the opposite hand rests on the forearm. There are some other variations of this sling that mount in a three-point fashion. I get a little confused by all of these as again everyone names the stuff after himself or herself. If possible, these three point types of slings should be reviewed or tested before purchase to see if they are going to work for you. Some people swear by them, others swear at them. The key is to have the sling set up at the proper swivel when needed.

Fig. 17.3

Military loop slings, although seen less today, are still a very viable tool. The military loop slings require some set up or loop up time for use, but it is usually time well spent. If a military loop sling is mounted correctly to a solid rifle stock, it can help the operator achieve a great deal of stability in firing positions. Because the sling is mounted securely to the stock, looped up tight and proper, excellent results can be achieved using it. (Fig. 17.3)

Cross body slings or what is referred to as tactical slings by many, are not really a new idea. As mentioned earlier, Calvary troops used them with success. Of this type, the best-designed and constructed sling is manufactured by Heckler & Koch and Blue Force Gear. The cross body sling allows a hands free mode while maintaining reasonable control of the primary weapon. Based on set up and fit, firing from the opposite shoulder in case of injury to the strong side can be difficult but it can be done and should be practiced by operators of the cross body sling weapons systems.   This style of sling can offer some assistance in weapon retention of the long gun in case of a physical struggle at short range. Refer to Section 11 and remember to rotate the rifle clockwise and lay it flat along the body with cross body slings (Fig. 17.4)

Fig. 17.4

BIPODS

Bipods can be a valuable asset in stabilizing the rifle in lowered (prone) or modified positions (resting over the hood of a car) where some elevation of the muzzle is needed. Bipods mounted to the rifle correctly should be attached to the forearm through the swivel eye or a stock mounted rail (Fig. 17.5). Bipods should not be mounted to the barrel, as attached to the rifle in this manner they *may* cause undue pressure on the barrel affecting the rifle's zero and projectile impact downrange.

Fig. 17.5

A recommended method of deployment calls for the operator, going to both knees, to open the strong side leg first, then the opposite leg while going down into position. As the operator starts to stand or recover return the legs to the up mode in reverse order of the way they were deployed.

My single biggest criticism of a bipod is that *many* operators use the bipod as a crutch. Without their bipod they are stuck in the "Well, I'm not stable enough to shoot" mode. A bipod is great, but you must be able shoot well with or without it! I had a student who went the whole week using his bipod off and on for various drills. On the last drill of the course, he was required to shoot from different positions at three targets from fifty yards to five hundred yards under duress. As he deployed the bipod for his five hundred yard shot the right leg *fell* off. He had a sad, sad look on his face! He looked at me for sympathy and you can guess my response. Stunned by my lack of "give a darn" he folded up the single leg, improvised a rest, fired and hit the target at five hundred yards. It was probably the highlight of his course. With all this information, I can go to the bottom line and tell you, in my opinion and on the range in application, the best bipod hands down of the whole lot for the AR platform is the Grip-Pod, Atlas Bipods are solid as well but take longer to deploy (Fig. 17.6).

Fig. 17.6

RETENTION STRAPS

Retention straps are about eighteen inches long with a solid snap on each end. In the stored mode, a snap is attached to each sling swivel. Its purpose is to secure the rifle from being lost or dropped from elevated platforms during deployment. Anytime my feet leave the ground, I unhook the snap from the front swivel and attach it to my web gear or harness. Why? In 1978, I was deployed on a S.W.A.T. call serving in the capacity of counter sniper. Over one hundred rounds had been fired prior to our deployment, so it was a hot place! I was assigned and deployed on a second story house roof made of a slate type material. In place, I had a good view and cover position to protect the anticipated point of entry for assault team. It started to rain (of course).   Looking through the scope while it was at rest, I noticed the cross wire moving off the area of the last place the suspect was seen. The cross wire seemed to move a little more and then all of the sudden it moved a lot as I started to slide down the now rain slick roof. I let go of the rifle as I slid down the roof sounding somewhat like a cat going across a chalkboard. If you are falling from the roof *you will let go of the rifle!* Fortunately, my feet caught hold near the gutter and I worked back to the seam of the roof, climbed back into position, threw a nylon strap around a roof pipe, and re-anchored. The rifle had remained crosswise so I was able to recover it. *Never again did I deploy in an elevated platform without attaching the rifle to me by use of the strap.* I think you get the point.

AMMUNITION

Ammunition can be selected by individuals or issued by agencies. There are many considerations in ammunition selection. Below are listed some of the more important points.

- The ammunition you select must function reliably. Period.

- You should test your selection or issue ammunition in all the types of mediums you think it may be deployed in. Examples may be sheet rock walls, car doors, glass and so on.

- Different bullet weights may need to be fired through the rifle to make sure bullet weights and rifle twists are compatible to achieve optimum accuracy.

- Most of the trouble, including the blowing up and complete destruction of a rifle, that I have seen in the last twenty- five years, comes from the use of reloaded ammunition.

- Make sure that the money you save by shooting reloads is worth the potential loss of your rifle. Don't shoot that imported crap ammunition.

- Based on whether or not your rifle is a pre or post ban rifle, it may or may not have a flash suppressor. Post ban rifles may not have a flash suppressor mounted on the barrel. Without a flash suppressor, there can be noticeably more muzzle signature or flash based on the type of ammunition you select. Since many confrontations occur in low or failing light, I would *test* the ammunition in a low or failing light environment to see what the muzzle signature is like.

SIGHTS

In section six I discussed what sights are, what they look like, and how to use them. Using the sights and manipulating the trigger correctly achieve optimum accuracy. The closer the threat is, the more important it is to stop them from doing whatever it is that made you decide to shoot them in the first place.

IRON

Although considered by many as archaic in today's world, iron sights should be available on any weapon you can possibly put them on. The true conditions of conflict create environments where rain, fog, dirt, injury or blood may obstruct sighting systems. These hostile environments may also flat out cause damage to the sights! Current Colt production rifles have two apertures available in an "L" type flip up configuration (Fig 17.7). There is a smaller, long-range aperture and a larger aperture for shorter ranges. Use of the smaller aperture restricts the field of view and constricts the available target and sighting area, but can reduce potential sighting errors. The larger aperture opens the field of view for both the target and surrounding area. My preference would be to use the larger aperture as much as possible to acquire the largest field of view and target. Threats usually move or are moving. The wider the field of view, the more likely you are to maintain target acquisition. For precision work or long range the smaller aperture is better. For fighting the larger aperture is best.

Fig. 17.7

SCOPES

The first thing to remember is that *"scopes do not help you shoot better, they only help you see better"*. Before someone gets hysterical, *seeing better can be very important!* However, even with a scope, the operator is still required to aim, hold, and squeeze the trigger correctly to get a hit. As with the iron sights, scopes can affect the field of view or what you see down range. The higher the power the narrower the field of view, the lower the power the more the field of view or what is available that you can see down range. With the Colt AR's, the high sight plane of the iron sights can make mounting a scope on top of the handle a strain or pain in the neck (Fig. 17.8). Flat top models (those without the carrying handle / iron sight removed) can lower the profile of the sight plane, ease neck strain and, *maybe most importantly, lower the profile of the operator's head while firing.*

Fig. 17.8

Any of the sights, Aimpoint T1 (Fig. 17.10), and Aimpoint CompM4 (Fig. 17.11) EoTechs, and ACOGs will work. I have seen all these scopes work and I have seen them all fail, but I have seen iron sights fail also. Some of these scopes require batteries so plan on carrying extra batteries everywhere. Battery life and dot technology is the best it has been. What used to be measured in hours of use is now measured in HUNDREDS of hours of use. Some models can be left on all year and not fail. I am aware of shelf life, half-life's etc. Question is, "Do I want to bet *my* life on a battery?" Some people do, some don't... or won't. Have extra batteries.

Fig. 17.10

Fig. 17.11

It becomes your call. Scopes that allow me to use the iron sights, even if the battery decides to be grumpy are my favorite. The argument then bottoms out at, "My scope has always worked. Why are you so opposed to them?" I am not opposed to them; I just don't want to bet my life on one. Then comes, "It's really fast." Maybe so... but I have never been to a fight that had a P.A.C.T. timer present. Think I am wrong? Next time you are at the range and you see a guy having a problem with a scoped anything ask him "What's the problem?" Bet you five bucks his reply is, "Well the damn scope this or that or whatever." It might well be the scope, but most problems are usually the operator. When it comes time to sort it out it goes like this: "The damn scope/ ammunition/ trigger/ barrel/ wind/ sun in my eyes, etc." My final comment is that you should have a rifle with iron sights that are zeroed correctly and work, and then you can add any additional sighting systems on the rifle you want to bet your life on. And put the scope on a good base the likes of American Defense Mfg. or GG&G or something. Lots of scopes take a dump based on crappy mounts!

LASERS

Lasers, batteries, well you already know what I think. Lasers with the dot are supposed to, at least in theory, psychologically intimidate the threat if the dot is on the threat's chest. Then the muzzle is also pointed at the chest. I am not going to point the muzzle at something I am not willing to destroy. If, I am going to destroy the threat, then shoot it, *which will psychologically intimidate them! If you're trying to just scare them put an ugly plastic mask on. It's cheaper than a lawyer!*

Infrared lasers and goggles (mostly limited to the military, or federal government, yeah, they don't even trust the local police) are very functional and effective. Interacting with different groups, I have had an opportunity to shoot these systems. I have effectively hit man size targets at 300 yards in total darkness. They do work; they are also battery dependent... and you know how I feel about betting my life on batteries.

FLASHLIGHTS

Many factors need to be considered when using a flashlight. The operator should use a flash light as little as possible while searching, enough to see but yet not enough to give your position away and become a beacon for incoming fire. Consider using the light in inconsistent patterns or sweeps to not set a trend for return fire. Using the current vogue strobe thing, the light could be used to blind a threat…. Then again, it won't affect their trigger finger or ability to shoot back. Option two is to use the light as much as possible to hold a known and found threat in place for the approach. Civilian applications might differ in that I may use a weapons mounted light to gain access to the light switch on the wall. Fighting in the light is much better than fighting in the dark. It is a good idea to see what you are about to press the trigger on. I don't know much about guns or shooting and I know less about kids, but if you shoot one of your children down the dark hallway ("I heard a noise") I think it will be a bad thing! By now you get the point; the use of the light is based on the potential threat, your environment, or your own personal opinion about how much danger you are in. Be careful on this ground.

WEAPON MOUNTED SYSTEMS

Most people's perception of a light failure is a light that won't come on. In the past, I have been more concerned with a weapon-attached light that is on and won't go off when I want it to. The weapons light market is mostly dominated, as it should be, by the best of the best, those being INSIGHT Tech Gear, Streamlight and Surefire in no order of preference (Fig. 17.12).

Fig. 17.12

Look for a system that has a pressure switch, off/on and maybe master override to enable/disable the system. After that, it is a simple choice of size, weight, and ease of operation. In the lights and fights mode, "one is none two is one." Streamlight Super-Tac's (Fig. 17.13) and Surefire X300 (Fig. 17.14) are personal favorites.

Fig. 17.13   Fig. 17.14

UN-MOUNTED LIGHTS

Effectiveness of hand held un-mounted lights is dependent upon size and weight of the weapon and physical conditioning to the operator. In Chapter 25, I will discuss techniques for using hand held lights.

NIGHT SIGHTS

Insert sights such as the Meprolight can be valuable assets to the rifle while sighting in low, altered or failing light. I personally prefer the front sight only, as I don't care for the illuminated sights close to my eye as it would be if the "dots" were mounted on the rear sight. By conditioning mounting of the rifle stock to your face (through repetition), the index of the stock sets up alignment of the front to rear sight. Some of the front sight "dots" are installed so that they may not be facing the correct way when the front sight is zeroed. Depending upon the degree of accuracy you require, you may have to rotate the sight so the "dot" is visible, but the rifle not correctly zeroed.

IMPROVISED SIGHTING

Many older veterans will be aware of the "painting or taping" of a white material to the front sight of the Colt AR type rifle to give a gross front sight. In this configuration, the "L" sight can be tipped to the half way so that neither aperture is available. Sighting is then accomplished by "looking" through the side rails that protect the rear sight while aligning the white front sight. This "sight" picture is then placed over the target. With practice, moving targets in lower light conditions can be hit reasonably well out to twenty-five yards. It is not a perfect technique, but can give reasonable results.

In Chapter 23, Night Firing Techniques there are more in depth descriptions and techniques.

Chapter 18

BARRICADES AND RESTS

Barricades are objects like cars or walls that come between you and the threat. They can provide cover, concealment or firing support for your rifle. Section 19 discusses barricades in a cover and concealment sense. In this section, the concern is the use of a barricade as a rest or support for the rifle.

The ultimate goal is to provide a stable platform from which the rifle can be fired. This stable platform goal can be achieved by using a proper firing position or by using a rest to support the rifle. If you can get steadier, ALWAYS get steadier. Don't stand if you can kneel; don't kneel if you can go to prone; and don't do any of these if you can rest the rifle on a support.

Some points of interest:

ALWAYS CLEAR THE MUZZLE BEFORE FIRING! ALWAYS CLEAR THE MUZZLE BEFORE FIRING! On some rifles like an AR the offset of the sights may be a lot higher than the barrel. Thus, you see the target through the sights but the muzzle is not clear of the barricade. **ALWAYS CLEAR THE MUZZLE BEFORE FIRING!** Get it? (Fig. 18.1).

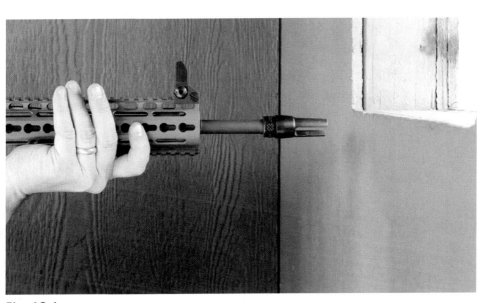

Fig. 18.1

Do not rest the rifle's barrel on the support. This contact can change the projectile's point of impact on the target (Fig. 18.2).

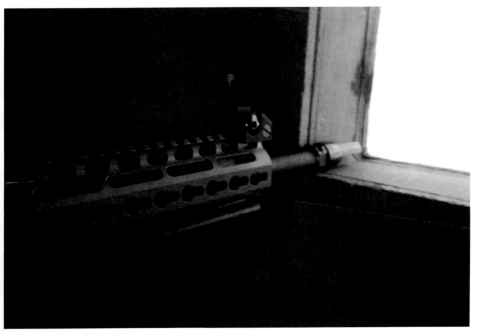

Fig. 18.2 (No)

Do not project the muzzle into an area not clear of potential threats [(Fig. 18.3) move to end of paragraph]. Examples could be doorways into uncleared rooms or around the corners of a building.

Fig. 18.3 (No)

In buildings or behind barricades, even when clear of threats, do not extend your hands or arms beyond the rest (Fig. 18.4). Incoming projectiles may fragment upon striking your cover or rest. These fragments can strike your exposed limbs causing injury.

Try to shoot around the sides of barricades and rests so as to limit the exposure of your head (Fig. 18.5). The head is a relatively vital body organ and will not hold up well to gunfire. Placing it above a rest of barricade makes it a good target. (Fig. 18.6)

Fig. 18.4 (No)

Fig. 18.5 (Yes)

Fig. 18.6 (No)

Try to stay in close to the barricade. If it is twelve inches wide for, example, stay as close to the protected edge as possible to limit your exposure. If the forearm of the rifle is resting horizontally on the barricade, you may want to move your opposite hand to the rear, grasping the toe of the stock by supporting the rear of the rifle in the pocket. (Fig. 18.7)

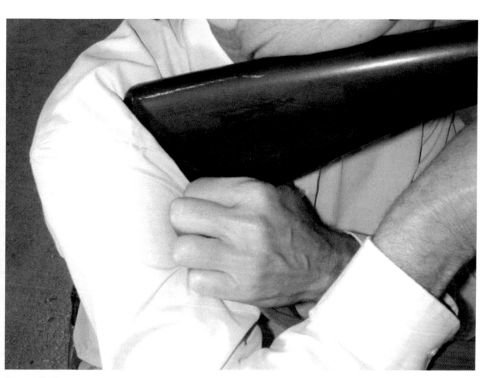

Fig. 18.7

Chapter 19

COVER AND CONCEALMENT

To properly discuss cover and concealment you should understand the difference between the two. Cover could be correctly called **shielding**, as it should stop, turn, impede or impair direct or indirect fire or fragmentation. Most of what makes up the world is not cover. It is, in fact, concealment. As a general guideline, it takes approximately thirty inches of loose soil to turn a .30 caliber round. Concrete walls (not celled cinder blocks) can stop rounds, but remember earlier comments about secondary fragmentation (Figs. 19.1, 19.2, 19.3).

Fig. 19.1

(*A projectile from an AK47 after passing through seven plywood walls inside a tactical house.*)

Fig. 19.2

(Penetration of .308 rounds through a rock wall from fifty yards away creating large amounts of secondary fragmentation.)

The majority of wounds I saw in the military were from secondary fragmentation. Those people I saw hit by direct rifle fire were usually in sad shape. They did not all necessarily die, but they were generally out of the fight. Please consider that the dynamics of your "cover" may change by what type of fire you are exposed to. You may start using cover down below and behind the vehicle door. Those incoming .38 caliber wad cutters may not be much of a threat. When your threat drops the revolver and switches to a 30-06 M-1 Garand, the dynamics of your choice of cover just changed (Fig. 19.3)
Regardless of the cover or concealment available, you are always better served to get behind something than to stand in the clear and receive direct fire.

Fig. 19.3
(*Large amounts of damage, even if not lethal, were done to the target behind the wall by secondary fragmentation.*)

Your opponents may use cover and concealment while directing fire at you. Your awareness of the potential of your cartridge against different concealment materials will help you deliver accurate and effective fire at the threat and through threat cover and concealment. Test your ammunition against different kinds of mediums to see what your projectiles will or won't pass through

Fig. 19.4

(Showing violence of action [but not penetration?] at the point of contact for the rifle rounds striking the wall. Note the large amount of debris in motion.)

I have had people tell me that their personal armor "won't stop rifle fire." We know armor may or may not stop rifle fire, and maybe it isn't supposed to. The armor is supposed to stop the secondary fragmentation created by the cover you get your arse behind! Use cover!

As was mentioned before, please use every opportunity to **shoot around protective cove**r, and concealment, **rather than over the top** of protection. Always reduce your head's exposure to gunfire.

You are better served to have as many materials or mediums as possible between you and incoming rounds!

Chapter 20

TARGET INDICATORS

Target indicators are not a new concept. Every single conflict has, had, or will have target indictors. The military is a traditional teacher of conflict target indictors. Whoever your teacher is, it is important for you to understand you cannot be involved in a conflict where target indicators are not present. The key is your personal awareness of your target indicators that will help reduce your individual projection of these target indicators to your opponent. Your awareness of the threat's target indicators and proper use of personal tactics will help you use the threat's target indicators to overcome the threat.

There are five primary target indicators and an additional one to consider.

1. SOUND

This can be the sounds of radio mikes being keyed, the rattle or "tink" of equipment, the shuffle of feet or the dragging of your body against the wall. Whichever it is, noise projects your presence or movement to the threat, if you choose to close with it. Your ability to be quiet and listen for the threat's movement or weapons manipulation could give you an idea of where it is or what the threat may be doing. This lead-time may give you a chance to prepare, to set up for a weapon response or a verbal compliance request.

2. MOVEMENT

Movement may be the most prolific or most easily recognized target indicator. My classroom example is, "If every deer in the woods stood still the first day of hunting season how many would get killed?" Movement deletes camouflage whether issued by God or Cabela's. With all of the talk about instinctive this or that, movement, or your eyes ability to pick up movement, may be one of the true instinctive capabilities of humans. This "skill" is sometimes called a "hunter's eye." It is reflected in contemporary firearms training by teaching students to watch for the threat's hands and hand movements. It is a fundamental training issue.

3. REFLECTION OR SHINE

Reflection or shine can come from many sources. Glare or flashes of light can come from the back of your hands, eyeglasses, scopes, wristwatch crystals, and even the "shine" of your face. This shine or flash of light can give away your position or movement to a threat's eyes, and can draw incoming fire. The masking or muting of shiny hands, a scope lens or equipment, should be an issue strongly addressed by operators to reduce potential indicators that can lead to operator injury.

4. CONTRAST

The quickest and most understandable example is a hunter wearing an orange vest in the woods. Other examples may be dark clothing moving in a light colored area of concrete buildings or a background of snow. In contrast, the white bathrobe of an armed homeowner coming down the hallway searching for an intruder works in the same negative way to make them a potential target.

5. OUTLINE

Outline can come from many things. Your bedroom light will cause you to be backlit as you enter a dark hallway. Movement in front of windows, either inside or outside the house, can outline your physical silhouette. Military doctrine teaches to stay off of skylines, rooflines, etc. This presentation of your silhouette will draw fire. Lower your profile. Reduce exposure time in doorways, stairwells and hallways to present less of a potential target. Reduce your outline and look for the threat's outline to increase your survivability.

6. SMELL

Depending on your occupation, smell may contribute to your ability to protect yourself from potential injury. In the private sector, if you enter your home and are greeted by the smell of natural gas it might be a good idea to get out. Exit the house and call the appropriate services to solve your problem. If I was a law enforcement officer assigned to a clandestine lab entry into a home or area with the strong smell of methane or ether, it may cause me some concern, especially if I thought there was a potential for the discharging of firearms to take place. It might be a bigger boom than we thought if we fire a small arm inside the house or structure filled with flammables.

Chapter 21

CAMOUFLAGE

Camouflage is an integral part of nature. Many, in fact most, animals that inhabit the earth have some kind of camouflage that protects them from predators. Camouflage can be seen in the stripes of a moving herd of zebras that serve to confuse attacking lions and a nesting mother bird's coloration that makes it hard for roving marauders to pick up on.

Camouflage works in three ways to help us:

1. **Hide or hiding**

Camouflage by coloration or by shape hides us from our opponent's view. By altering our natural color to match that of our surroundings, we can hide more easily from prying eyes. Examples could be camouflage clothing to hide and blend in the jungle or an unmarked police car parked over the next hill.

2. **Blend or blending**

Camouflage by blending in the environment we occupy by matching coloration or changing the human outline or shape reduces the ability of potential threats to see us. Examples could be camouflage clothing, plain clothes police officers or unmarked police cars.

3. **Deceive or deception**

Camouflage by deception is the art of looking like something I am not. Examples could be the infamous "Q" ships of WW I or WWII. These "innocent looking" freighters were actually well armed ships with a façade that allowed them to close with unarmed Allied merchant vessels. An exotic example is the "dazzle" painted surface warships whose paint schemes altered the outline of these vessels to the inquisitive eyes of submariners or opposition gun crews. A field example is the bushy outline altering Ghillie suits designed by Scottish gamekeepers.

The whole concept of camouflage is to hide us from, make us blend in with, or deceive potential opponents of the fact of who or where we are.

Chapter 22

MOVEMENT

The discussion of movement while fighting always brings up a flurry of opinions. The more logical conversations come from people with practical experience in actual conflict. Most of the difficulties of movement are well recognized. We often hear, "I don't shoot as well when I'm moving," followed by, "A real man stands on his two legs and fights" and so on.

Food for thought

Ask yourself, if you were going to be shot at in three seconds would you stand still or move to cover? Do you think your threat will stand still or move if you shoot at them? The people you fight may be dumb, but they are probably not stupid. A subtle point here, the longer the fight lasts the more danger you are in because, eventually, you'll be fighting smart people since all the stupid ones got killed.... The same goes for our side.

Of all the rounds of ammunition you have ever fired, what percentage did you fire while shooting at a stationary target compared to moving targets? Where has most of your practice been? As a point of interest, if you watch cop dash cams in gunfights it looks like lots of people move around in gunfights!

Using the concept that a step forward is forward movement, a step back is back, left is left and right is right, try correctly clearing the bedroom doorway and down the hall into your living room. Remember to "pie" the angles to minimize your exposure as you go. You should quickly see that there is a great deal of lateral and back movement to reduce over-exposure while you work down the hallways and around corners. The actual movements while progressing forward mostly come from lateral movement.

Forward movement is okay, but remember you are closing ground with a potentially life threatening entity. When I go down a hallway with a firearm looking for a potential threat with a firearm, this is a lot like closing ground with a running chainsaw looking for someone with a running chainsaw. It might be pretty exciting when the two saws meet!

One of the basics of movement is to remember to keep your feet somewhat apart to provide a stable base. The shifting of body weight to one foot so that the "light" foot can be moved and reset must preface any movement. It generally works best to lead into the direction of movement with the foot that is closest to the direction we want to go. Moving to the right, I would move the right foot first and then bring along the left to reestablish the firing platform.

In rearward movement or withdrawals you should still lead with the strong foot. While placing the strong foot to the rear, make an attempt to "feel" where you are going with your toe before shifting your weight and putting your heel down. When the strong foot is down, recover the opposite foot to a firing platform. *Always remember almost any threat can come at you forward faster than you can back up. I am backing up in this fashion not for speed, but so as to maintain a firing platform to shoot from while I back up.* Graveyards are full of people who wouldn't back up...like George Custer.

If you look at history, when it comes to backing up, true killing in combat doesn't really begin until one side turns to run from the fray. That's when lots of people really get killed. Keep your gun towards the threat and open the ground if required. When the threat is close, the thought comes to mind "He's so close I can't miss." This should be replaced with, "He's so close I better not miss."

Your foot should not be connected to the trigger. In others words, I don't fire every time my right or left foot contacts the ground. I fire when I have a good sight picture on a threat I am willing to shoot. Learning to shoot and move is not always an easy skill to grasp. It is an acquired skill based on repetition and diligent practice.

Chapter 23

NIGHT FIRING TECHNIQUES

It is pretty well documented that a reasonably large percentage of gunfights take place in altered or low light environments. You should do the best you can to try to participate in night, low, or altered light training. After doing the firearms training thing for a few decades, I have found the best way to teach night fire training is by starting in the daylight. Confirm all manipulation skills such as loading and malfunction clearance and the physical act of turning the lights off and on. By polishing skills with weapons mounted or handheld light techniques, it makes the "in the dark stuff" much easier to apply in real life.

A helpful training point is to have a simulator that allows low or no light environments that can be used in the daylight hours. For training applications closer to home, maybe approaching the local indoor range owners and seeing if you can talk them into lowering the lights for some firing. This can help provide you with valuable exposure to low light training. Where there is a will there is a way... most of the time.

The primary focus of this section is to provide the reader with some introductory techniques and concepts to applying a rifle to a fight in altered light environments. These are not my ideas and I didn't invent anything or name anything after myself. These concepts come from many places, over many years of exposure. They may or may not work for you based on environment, application, occupation or experience.

Most rifle fights take place inside what could be considered pistol range. Rifle shooters will probably be moving to find cover, out of the line of fire, or to get better target acquisition. Threats may be moving for the same reasons. The fight won't be what you want it to be. It could be dark, quick and ugly. Since AR-15's are so prolific, I will address them, but all of these techniques are transferable to other weapons systems. Try them all. Use what works for you.

Large Apertures

Most AR's currently come with a large and small aperture. In the Vietnam era, these larger sight apertures became available, but in eighteen months in the country circa 68-69, I personally did not see one mounted on a rifle. The larger aperture is better because it allows a wider field of view and the rear sight obstructs less down range. The small aperture is more accurate in precision shooting and for longer ranges. The larger aperture requires some work to be accurate at mid and longer ranges. Most fights take place at short range and with moving threat targets. The best way to use this type of sight is a proper butt placement to the shoulder and cheek weld. Look at the sights superimposed over the threat and hit them. Only hits count. Another point is that the iron sights never run out of battery power.

Tipped Sights

If the light is bad, and it may be—and the range is short, and it may be— say twenty-five yards or so, this technique works with practice. Tip the rear sight so that it is half way between the large and small aperture settings. Using the outside edges of the carrying handle (which protects the rear sight) as a guide, look at the front sight.

Keep the butt correctly placed in the shoulder pocket and get a correct cheek weld to make sure you have correct alignment of the rifle. The outside edges of the rear sight protector serve as the rear sight and the whole front sight assembly serves as the front sight. In altered light, it is not unusual to not be able to see the front sight post but still be able to see the front sight assembly. This works on gross moving targets at shorter ranges. It is not for precision shooting. In actual fact, you are simply looking over the rear sight at the front sight assembly. You maintain a proper cheek weld to minimize tipping the front sight so high that projectiles go over the top of the threat. Perfect? No! It is, however, functional with practice and applied in the correct place it works. You can apply the same technique without tipping the rear sight after you program yourself to *look just above the rear sight* while finding/focusing on the front sight assembly. This is a short-range failing light technique, at best. It requires modest practice to even get the idea of doing it correctly. In reality, it may not work for you at all.

Tape it or Paint It?
Using the above technique, the rear face of the front sight assembly can be highlighted with paint or white medical tape to help you get a better visual on the front sight assembly. This paint/tape adds a great deal to the effectiveness of this technique. I try to mark and use the top inch of the front sight. Before the tape/paint concept was applied, in one particular application in Vietnam, there were several of those other people moving laterally from left to right across our front at about fifteen to twenty-five yards. There was a bunch of rifle fire applied, both aimed and un- aimed without much success. In a daylight review it appears that we "killed' many trees at the six to ten foot height range from ground level. This wasn't really bad except we weren't trying to hit the trees and the "little" people were well below the line of fire. Yeah, I know hand grenades and claymores... learn as you go. We added the tape first and then the paint as it stuck better in that unfriendly climate.

Weapons Mounted Illumination
Because of job requirements or your occupation you may have to illuminate the potential threat to confirm weapons, and correctly ID suspects. Private sector people need to confirm weapons and be in fear of their life—and be able to convince the grand jury that they were, in

fact, in fear of their life—and be ready to hire a lawyer. With that said we can go on.

There is a huge disagreement in place over how illumination and weapons using lights should be applied. First and foremost, the user should understand that there are, in reality, two light sources... the spot of light choreographed or aligned with the muzzle, and the arc of light surrounding the spot provided by today's high tech light systems. This learning process parallels the "tunnel vision" concept — generally the user will look at the spot and directing the spot they thereby point the muzzle in all kinds of directions and places that may not be appropriate. This was illustrated and litigated with incidents where cops were pointing weapons mounted lights and the muzzles at people during regular DL checks. The user should train to use the eyes to clear, work, search, scan, and identify within the arc of light surrounding the spot and then, if required, bring the spot and hence the muzzle on target, if verbal compliance requests are not adhered to and gunfire is required to solve the problem.

Tactical Nuances

- If it has batteries or a bulb, plan on it not working when you need it.
- If you need a flashlight you had better have two.
- Your light, solid or strobe, may impair your threat's eyesight but it won't do anything to his trigger finger.

There are many good weapons mounted light systems on the market today. Streamlight (Fig. 23.1), Surefire (Fig. 23.2) and Insight are some of the best. I have seen light bulbs fail in these systems. L.E.D's seem to be more reliable. Then again, a light bulb in your house doesn't last forever and neither do automobile head lights. *The issue is not if they don't work, but what I do if they don't work.* Remember, tools in the toolbox. Train to the fact the rifle may work but the flashlight won't. Train to the fact that the flashlight may work and the rifle won't. Train to the fact that the light may come on, and because of it I am drawing incoming fire; and perhaps the light won't go off when I need it to. You get the point!

Fig. 23.1

The Rifle and Hand Held Techniques

With practice and exposure all of the current handgun flashlight techniques will work for the rifle. Some techniques may require a slight modification based on the rifle size and weight, or the users upper body strength. So buff up if you plan on doing a lot of rifle work. Much of the work here is not about muscle as much as it is tone...using the muscles you have to support the firing process.

Fig. 23.2

Fig. 23.3

Crossed

Using the same technique as you would with a handgun, the crossed wrist technique contacts and supports the underside of the forearm on the rifle. The flashlight hand elbow may be required to be slightly higher than with a handgun to help support rifle weight. As with the handgun, this technique works great for everything except clearing hard right corners. This resembles the old Harries technique (Fig. 23.3)

Uncrossed

Using this technique requires the user to have decent upper body strength. In this method, the operator simply uncrosses the wrist from under the forearm of the rifle and has the flashlight held parallel to the rifle barrel alongside the forearm. The reason you need more upper body strength is because, in reality, you are holding the rifle with one hand. A cure for this is to roll the flashlight hand outboard and let the heel of the hand slide under and support to rifle forearm (Fig. 23.4). This is a quick fix to the overexposure of the user on right hand corners. As the user approaches the right hand corner in the crossed technique, simply uncross, minimizing body and head exposure as you clear the right corner. Once clear and around the corner, the user can cross under the forearm and reacquire wrist contact and support for the front of the rifle.

Fig. 23.4

Syringe

Upper body strength together with the weight of rifle can affect the syringe technique. The syringe requires a flashlight with a rear activation button. With this technique, the strong hand and arm are holding the rifle while the opposite hand holds the light alongside the forearm of the rifle. By applying rearward pressure with the fingers, the light button is activated by the base of the hand (Fig. 23.5). This probably has lineage with Bill Rogers.

Fig. 23.5

Syringe Supported

The light is in the same location alongside the forearm as in the syringe technique, but the change is that some of the lower fingers of the support hand holding the light are extended to contact the underside of the forearm so there is some support for the rifle (Fig. 23.6). I personally like this technique best when it fits the world I am working in. This has lineage to Bill Rogers and Mas Ayoob.

Fig. 23.6

Magazine Well Contact

The MWC is a good combination of support for the rifle and the flashlight. In this technique, which requires there either be no sling or that the sling is moved out of the way of the underside of the rifle forearm, the rifle is held by the strong hand and the flashlight is centered under the rifle with the opposite hand. The flashlight with a rear-mounted switch is compressed by the left hand rearward so that pressing against the front of the magazine well activates the switch. This turns the light on for searching, and forward movement of the hand releases pressure letting the light turn off. In the process, the opposite hand is helping to support the weight of the rifle (Fig. 23.7). Ted Funetes was the first guy I saw use this technique in a class.

Fig. 23.7

Muzzle Signature or Flash

As a thought, please make an attempt to shoot your rifle in low or no light environments to see for yourself what kind of muzzle signature or "flash" you project (Fig. 23.8). The people you encounter may be dumb, but they probably won't be stupid. When you fire, if you have excessive muzzle flash, there is a strong likelihood that people can and will shoot at this signature. Shoot and test as many kinds of ammunition as you can so that you can get what works best in your rifle (Fig. 23.8). Pre-ban and post-ban barrels with flash reducers or a barrel without a flash reducer can project extremely different kinds of signatures. In personal testing, the Vortex hiders have worked best for me using regular ball ammunition.

Fig. 23.8

Night Vision Equipment

The ability to see in the dark, in my opinion, has value not so much that it allows me to fight as it would be to allow me to break or avoid contact to start with. If you are in a solid or fixed position and cannot or will not move due to position advantage, family or injury or a combination of these things, then the NVD's, especially high quality equipment, will allow you to engage target at modest ranges. Wife Heidi, using her PVS14 (Fig. 23.9) and a Noveske N4 rifle, consistently thumps targets to three hundred yards. I have tested equipment for GG&G and American Defense

Mfg. and would recommend their NVD systems and bases if you want an NVD capability (Fig. 23.10).

Own the Night You may or may not own the night, but fighting in the dark is highly overrated and often discussed by people who haven't done it. It would be wise to put altered light rifle firing techniques with both handheld and weapons mounted illumination systems into your toolbox of basic skills. ***BEFORE YOU NEED THEM!***

Fig. 23.9

Fig. 23.10

Chapter 24

CARE AND CLEANING

The Rifleman's Creed

"This is my rifle. There are many like it, but this one is mine.

My rifle is my best friend. It is my life. I must master it as I must master my life.

My rifle, without me, is useless. Without my rifle, I am useless. I must fire my rifle true. I must shoot straighter than my enemy who is trying to kill me. I must shoot him before he shoots me. I will...

My rifle and I know that what counts in this war is not the rounds we fire, the noise of our burst, nor the smoke we make. We know that it is the hits that count. We will hit...

My rifle is human, even as I, because it is my life. Thus, I will learn it as a brother. I will learn its weaknesses, its strength, its parts, its accessories, its sights and its barrel. I will keep my rifle clean and ready, even as I am clean and ready. We will become part of each other. We will...

Before God, I swear this creed. My rifle and I are the defenders of my country. We are the masters of our enemy. We are the saviors of my life.

So be it, until victory is America's and there is no enemy, but peace!"

Major General William H. Rupertus

Although this may seem a bit brash to some, there are a few very subtle messages in this creed. I have seen hundreds of rifles over the years butchered by gunsmiths and students alike, to meet some criteria they imagine to exist.

Get a rifle. Zero it. Shoot it and don't screw with it! If it doesn't work get rid of it and get one that meets the standard you perceive you need. *As far as actual field application, I can't think of a scenario or problem **that a rifle that shot inside two inches at 100 yards** would not have solved!* With this degree of accuracy it means **the rifle is capable of hitting a ten-inch paper plate at 500 yards!**

Consider two things:

1. Intrinsic accuracy- potential mechanical accuracy of the rifle.

2. Practical accuracy- accuracy achieved with the operator attached to the rifle.

Accurate rifles are great, they are fun to shoot; those that have one really like it. **But I don't know if will make a difference in a fight**. Get a factory manual for your rifle and care for it as the manufacturer recommends. Who built more rifles, you or Remington? Rifles are, of course, mechanical devices. Mechanical devices break or they can be assembled incorrectly. Rifles may need adjustment. If yours needs adjustment take it to a *competent* gunsmith.

About now you are wondering why we are in this mode in a section on care and cleaning?
Because the accuracy everyone is so concerned about is directly related to the way the rifle is maintained and taken care of. Sort of like a computer, garbage in garbage out.

Points to consider:

- Get <u>good</u> cleaning equipment, rods, brushes, patches, etc. They should be the best you can afford.

- Clean your rifle from the chamber end using a bore guide. If you use rifles like M-1 Garands or old Winchester lever action rifles, these are required to be cleaned from the front end. On these types of rifles, use a muzzle /crown bore guide protector to align the cleaning rod in the center of the bore to reduce potential damage. So you know, the crown is the final release point for the projectile as it leaves the rifle muzzle. If is dented or damaged it can affect the way the projectile is released from the muzzle, altering the yaw of the projectile as goes down range, which can effect accuracy.

- Learn how to and where to lubricate the operating parts. I have seen students put just short of a quart of 10w40 into the actions. When the rifle action reciprocates upon firing, there is a spray of smoking oil that covers the face and glasses. Oil it yes, but drown it in oil? NO! Some systems don't like oil. The Garand, for example, prefers a more grease like compound for lubrication of the bolt. Research information about the rifle you own. If your rifle is of military origin, obtain the military manuals regarding your type of weapon and see what the people who used it most have to say about taking care of it.

- If you use a bolt action, listed below is one correct way to break in a new rifle barrel and clean your rifle on a daily basis. These recommendations come from Robbie Barkman formerly of ROBAR, Inc. Phoenix AZ.

NEW RIFLE BREAK IN

For the best results and long life of your rifle barrel, we suggest the following break-in procedure:

1. Thoroughly clean the barrel <u>before</u> starting to shoot. We recommend a good quality brass brush, a coated cleaning rod, a quality bore guide and a brass jag with soft clean patches. For solvents we recommend Shooters Choice.

2. Clean the barrel from the chamber end. First, using a bore guide, a brass brush and plenty of solvent, scrub the barrel well and wipe down with several soft clean patches. When the above procedure has been completed and a patch comes out clean, proceed to the first shot from your new barrel. The barrel must be dry internally.

3. Fire one round only and follow the above procedure for a total of ten rounds, thoroughly cleaning between each shot.

4. When you have completed this initial single shot sequence, you may proceed to the next step, two shots and clean, for a total of twenty rounds or ten sets of two. You must clean after every two rounds. At no time should the barrel be allowed to get so hot that you are unable to hold it comfortably in your hand.

WARNING: Do not use any kind of abrasive cleaner in the bore of your rifle.

For the best accuracy and long life of your rifle barrel we recommend that you clean the barrel after every five rounds. You can never over clean your rifle barrel. You should never go beyond ten rounds without cleaning. By keeping the barrel clean and only using good quality ammunition you should get years of service and supreme accuracy from your rifle. Never leave solvent in the barrel for extended periods.

Another Point of View
All this being said, a rifle is made to shoot and there is a train of thought that all this cleaning removes the "cure" from the barrel like in the old days of cast iron frying pans. I have seen people clean the rifles in excess and I'm not sure that they didn't damage it by over cleaning. I think if you shoot the rifle regularly, like a couple of times a week like I can here at Thunder Ranch in Oregon, then just patching it might be okay. If I planned on storing the rifle for the next few months, then I may clean it a bit more and run an oil patch through the bore. With my own eyes I have seen rifles shoot very well over long periods of time without the excessive cleaning that even I might have recommended in years past. Bottom line, your equipment is expensive you should maintain it as you believe or know to be correct.

Chapter 25

RANGE DRILLS

It is my opinion that, whenever possible, range practice should be conducted similar to Boy Scout swimming lessons... you should do it in a buddy system format. Going to the range and practicing with a buddy is beneficial in that your buddy can help you set up range drills, provide you with someone to set up malfunctions, monitor your gun handling and above all else provide you with assistance if something goes wrong. It might be a long crawl to the car and an even longer drive to the hospital. Many people disagree with this thought, so to each his own.

First and foremost:
Apply the four firearms safety rules anytime you practice or handle any firearm (chapter 2, pg. 11).

Start your range drills with a careful examination of the bore to make sure it is clear of any obstructions. Confirm the zero of your rifle. In layman's terms, put the sights on the center of the target, fire and see where the projectile strikes the target. For example, on most modern calibers like .223, .308, .30-06 a sight held on center of the target at 100 yards will give you approximately the following:

Caliber	100 yards	200 yards	300 yards
.223 55-grain	point of aim point of impact zero	-4" low	-12" low
.308 150-grain	point of aim point of impact zero	-4" low	-14" low
.30-06 150-grain	point of aim point of impact zero	-4" low	-15" low

This can vary based on bullet weight, but will hold to this scale reasonably well. If you use a cannon size charge of powder, a very lightweight projectile, or the wind is blowing gale force, this scale can vary at 300 yards. The point is, if you held center of mass —a horizontal line under the armpits—on a man size target from zero to 300 yards, you hit in the torso. Even at 300 yards, the projectile would strike the groin on a standing man.

If you change to a 200 yard zero, point of aim point of impact, you can see the scale below to get a concept of the difference. These are approximate, but you get the idea:

Caliber	100	200	300
.223 55-grain	+2.5	zero	-9"
.308 150-grain	+3"	zero	-9"
.30-06 150-grain	+3"	zero	-9"

In my opinion, a 200 yard zero would be good all-around zero for hunting in the field or basic defensive use. A 200 yard zero may not be all that great for a law-enforcement officer working in a big city environment, but then again some degree of common sense is required in all of this.

Drills
Gun fighting is often like family vacations; in the end they do not always pan out the way we thought they would in the beginning. Your range drills should combine a mixture of the basic skills you think you'll need to know with some skills that are a little harder to acquire. Remember, a fight won't be what you want. It will be what it is! These drills may need to be modified to address the range you have to work on.

Zero or confirm your zeroed range as mentioned above.

Training Point!
Work on good trigger control in the whole program and activate the safety off and on during the drills so you remember to turn the damn thing off and on at the correct time. You don't train with the safety to be safe. It is good to be safe, but the reason is to train so you don't forget the safety in a fight... and get killed because of it! About now it would cross your mind to just take the safety off and leave it off. I could go with this, except how many gunfights have you been in and how many times have you tripped and fallen? Which have you done more of? In the *safety off* mode, how many people do you know you would trust with their safety off behind you in a fight?

Position Shooting
Apply the three primary firing positions without support.

1. **Offhand**

2. **Kneeling:** Remember there are three: braced, quick and speed. Work all three.

3. **Prone:** Real men stand and shoot; *they also get shot if they stand in the wrong place too long.*

Shoot five slow fire singles for accuracy from each position first.
This stresses accuracy, proper position assumption and natural point of aim. Try to call your shots as you fire.

Shoot five pairs (aimed fire) from each position.
These drills stress accuracy and follow through shots, in case your target doesn't respond with one shot.

Shoot these drills from 5, 10 15, 25, 50, 75 and 100 yards if the range allows.
By firing these drills at different ranges, you can see if there is much opening up of the groups as the range increases. The comparison is like a trumpet; at the closer ranges (the mouth piece) the errors may be there, but are not amplified by the extended (large end of the trumpet) range.

- You can repeat the above with loop slings and then, again, with a bipod if required.

- With a loop sling you are more solid, but you are "tied" to the rifle.

- With a bipod you are more stable in prone, but there could be a price paid in set up time. This is very minimal if you use a Grip-Pod bipod system.

These ranges can be extended, but understand, as the range increases the higher your head is from the ground the larger the group. It's simple. In standing, the greater the range the bigger the group gets. As the range increases, lower your profile to gain stability. This also reduces your profile as a potential target.

Shoot the above drills using a representative barricade that can simulate cover and/or concealment, and yet provide a rest where appropriate. Remember to stay as close to the angle of the cover as possible in the sense that the forearm of the rifle is tucked tight into the corner to minimize the exposure of your head. *People shoot at you because they can see you, and they hit you because you let them see you.* Also, remember that you do not have to physically go to the cover to have it protect you. It simply needs to be between you and the incoming fire. A point of interest, try to avoid having any part of your body forward of the protective cover. Incoming rounds, even ones that miss you, will create secondary fragmentation when they strike your cover. This creates rocks, metal jacketing and lead cores. All of this stuff can give you wounds that are dangerous and harmful.

Loading & reloading drills
As stated before, there are two types of loading: empty loads and tactical loads. These loads are explained in detail in Section 15. Practice both types of loads equally. If I were personally going to favor one over the other, I would lean towards the empty load. Repetition being the mother of skill, you cannot practice these loading drills too much. Do it until it is right, and then do it some more!

Malfunctions
There are many reasons that a rifle will malfunction. I don't care what they are and neither will you in the middle of a fight. Each range session should include as many variations of potential malfunctions as you can produce. It is best to have another shooter set up the malfunction so you don't know what to expect. You simply clear the problem and go on.

A point of interest: do not place loaded rounds into the chamber and then attempt to chamber a second loaded cartridge. It will create a double feed, and it might also allow the pointed end of the second cartridge to strike the primer of the chambered round causing a detonation of that round while the bolt is open. Bad business! To set up this drill lock the bolt to the rear on a loaded magazine. Then place an empty case on top of the rounds in the magazine then slowly ease the charging handle and bolt forward. This will load the live round from magazine but wedge the empty case at the feed ramp and make the "V" safely.

It is also best not to put empty cases into the chamber, as these fired cases sometimes wedge very tightly into the chamber, and are a real pain to clear. In action, empty cases could be found in the chamber with the bolt to the rear. The extractor hook has either broken or jumped the case rim. The magazine needs to be removed and the bolt reciprocated. Even this action may not clear the chamber, and a transition to your secondary firearm may be in order.

Transition drills
You already know why and where you would transition to a second working firearm. In practice, MAKE SURE THE WEAPON TO BE DISCARDED IS EMPTY. The proper set up is to have a rifle staged with one round in the magazine, chamber that round and remove the magazine. Ensure that the rifle magazine is removed. On command attempt to fire the rifle TWO times. So the drill should go: command to FIRE, bang, click (the hammer falls on an empty chamber). Then, transition to the working firearm. It is imperative that the rifle be empty when it is moved into the transition mode. By setting up the drill this way it ensures the rifle will be empty after the first round is fired. It is imperative that you press the trigger for the second round on the rifle. Your indicator that the rifle is not functioning is the "CLICK" of the trigger on the empty chamber. This will be an audible as well physical indicator that the rifle is out of service. In some styles of transitions, the defunct rifle muzzle is moved laterally or towards the firing line. It must be empty! After the "threat" has been engaged, the clearing or rearming of the rifle, if possible, would complete the drill.

Injury drills
Injury drills should be conducted with a "safety buddy" because of potential muzzle movement. Operators should practice loading and unloading with the opposite (weak) hand as well as firing the rifle

135

opposite handed and opposite eye (non-dominate) to get full value out of the practice. The "safety buddy" monitoring the muzzle should kneel next to the shooter to keep their upper body and head out of the line of fire in case the muzzle should slide down the rest or support being used as cover for the drill. It is also advisable for the "safety buddy" to be alert for ejecting brass if they are kneeling on the right side of the shooter. The ejecting brass can strike the safety person in the face if care is not taken.

Moving & wobbling targets
The simplest of moving targets can be of great value. The threat will move if they get a chance. Learn to shoot movers now... *not in the middle of a fight.* If you lack moving targets, colored balloons suspended up from strings by helium or down by gravity, work well in a light breeze. The shooter shoots the color balloon called out by your range buddy. Don't hit the wrong color!

Movement
The range you work on may regulate the amount of movement you can do in practice. At the very least take one right, left, or back step to program movement to position. Moving from standing to kneeling or prone also works to practice set up as well as increasing your heart rate after eight to ten repetitions. You can run and jump if you like, but a little of that stuff goes a long way. In the old days at Gunsite on the Scrambler course, or currently here at Thunder Ranch on the Thunderville rifle tactical run, a distance of about 80 feet, most folks are ready to throw up upon completion of the run. There's nothing personal in this, just a fact. *Learn to shoot well... so you don't have to run as far.*

Low light drills
If you could shoot low light drills every time you went to the range, you still wouldn't get *too much* practice. Most fights take place in low or altered light environments. Your practice should address things you know you might encounter. There is enough stuff we don't know about, but there is no sense avoiding what statistics tell us. Fighting in the daylight is tough... at night it can flat out get ugly. With reduced vision and moving targets, threat and threat weapon identification can be difficult at best. Civilians and Law Enforcement officers need to clarify weapons and threats. Military personnel could seem to have it better "We're here,

they are over there," but high friendly fire causality rates seem to dictate otherwise. You need to practice to reduce some degree of the stress involved in these altered light engagements. Pre-conditioned programmed skill begets competency. ***Train hard, fight easier!?!?***

Dismounts

You will always carry a rifle more than you will fight with it. You may shoot a rifle more in practice than you shoot it in anger. In that vein, the practicing of dismounts should be worked to some degree in every practice session.

Thoughts

- Apply safety and safe handling habits to practice.
- Check the zero on your rifle.
- Shoot as much short range (0-25 yards) as you do long (25-to whatever range).
- Remember, practice and apply the rifle to all ranges and sizes of targets, always considering the mechanical off-set of the sights. If the rifle is zeroed for 100 yards, and the shot I need to take is five yards away, where do I hold and more importantly where will the projectile strike?
- "I was here. I was close. I had the will, and I killed the hostage." It has an odd ring to it don't you think?

In closing, I would like to recommend and thank some of the companies and individuals that have helped us along the way with firearms, optics, rifles, targets, and ammunition. They have stood by us for years and continue to assist us in moving forward. We could not do what we love without their continued support and products.

Action Target

Aimpoint

Carroll Pilant, Sierra Bullets

Chad Long, GPS Arms

Chris Hodgdon, Hodgdon Powder

EuroOptics

Garth Kendig, Leupold

George Gardner, G.A. Precision

Jason Burton, Heirloom Precision

Jeff Hoffman, Black Hills Ammunition

Kasey Beltz, B&T Ind. / Atlas

Les Baer

Mossberg

Noveske Rifleworks

Rick Johnson, Remington

Sheri Johnson, EraThr3

Tony Miele, Smith & Wesson

Made in the USA
Middletown, DE
20 November 2021